Security Book!

Alex T. Rimms

Copyright and Legal Statement

© 2024 by Alex T. Rimms

All rights reserved. No part of this book may be reproduced, distributed, or transmitted in any form or by any means, including photocopying, recording, or other electronic or mechanical methods, without the prior written permission of the publisher, except in the case of brief quotations embodied in critical reviews and certain other noncommercial uses permitted by copyright law.

The information contained in "Security Book" is for informational purposes only. While every effort has been made to ensure the accuracy and completeness of the information provided, the author and publisher make no representations or warranties of any kind, express or implied, about the completeness, accuracy, reliability, suitability, or availability with respect to the contents of this book for any purpose. Any reliance you place on such information is therefore strictly at your own risk.

The topics covered in "Security Book," including Security and Encryption, Privacy and Online Safety, Hacking, Networking and Cloud Computing, Certification, Viruses and Malware, Food Safety and Security, Social Security and Welfare, and Freedom and Security, are intended to provide general information and guidance. Readers are encouraged to seek professional advice and consult relevant authorities or experts in specific situations or circumstances.

The inclusion of any third-party resources, websites, or tools in this book does not imply endorsement or recommendation by the author or publisher. Users are responsible for evaluating and utilizing such resources at their own discretion and risk

"Security Book" is a work of non-fiction and does not contain any fictional elements or characters. Any resemblance to actual persons, living or dead, or actual events is purely coincidental.

For permissions, inquiries, or feedback regarding "Security Book," please contact the publisher.

Thank you for respecting the intellectual property and legal rights associated with "Security Book."

Alex T. Rimms

"Security Book"

Chapter: Introduction to Security 8

Chapter: Exploring Different Types of Security Threats 11

Chapter: Security and Encryption 14

Chapter: Implementing Strong Encryption Practices 17

Chapter: Privacy and Online Safety 20

Chapter: Safeguarding Against Identity Theft and Fraud 23

Chapter: Hacking Demystified 26

Chapter: Techniques and Tools Used in Ethical Hacking 29

Chapter: Networking and Cloud Computing Security 32

Chapter: Best Practices for Cloud Security 36

Chapter: Certification for Security Professionals 40

Chapter: Advancing Your Career in the Security Field 44

Chapter: Viruses and Malware 48

Chapter: Steps to Take in Case of a Malware Attack 52

Chapter: Food Safety and Security 55

Chapter: Preventing Contamination and Ensuring Food Security 59

Chapter: Social Security and Welfare 63

Chapter: Safeguarding Social Welfare Programs Against Fraud 66

Chapter: Freedom and Security 70

Chapter: Privacy vs. Surveillance: Debates and Considerations 73

Chapter: The Future of Security 77

Chapter: Empowering Readers to Stay Safe and Secure in an Evolving World 81

BONUS CHAPTERS 85

Chapter: Encryption 85

Chapter: Cryptographic Algorithms 89

Chapter: Data Protection 93

Chapter: Cybersecurity 97

Chapter: Cryptography 101

Chapter: Information Security 105

Chapter: Information Security 109

Chapter: Secure Communication 113

Chapter: Encryption Techniques 117

Chapter: Encryption Protocols 120

Chapter: Encryption Standards 123

Chapter: Symmetric Encryption 126

Chapter: Asymmetric Encryption 129

Chapter: Encryption Keys 132

Chapter: Key Management 135

Chapter: Data Encryption 139

Chapter: Encryption Software 142

Chapter: Network Security 146

Chapter: Cryptography Basics 150

Chapter: Encryption Principles 153

Chapter: Secure Coding Practices 156

Chapter: Encryption in the Cloud 159

Chapter: Quantum Encryption 162

Chapter: Encryption for Beginners 166

Chapter: Bitcoin and Cryptocurrency Explained 169

Chapter: Introduction to Security

Understanding the Importance of Security in Today's Digital Age

In an era defined by interconnectedness and digital innovation, the concept of security has taken on newfound significance. From personal data protection to safeguarding critical infrastructure, the need for robust security measures permeates every aspect of our lives. In this chapter, we delve into the fundamental principles of security and explore why it is indispensable in our modern, technology-driven world.

The Evolution of Security:
We begin by tracing the evolution of security paradigms, from physical barriers and guards to sophisticated digital encryption and cyber defenses. The shift towards digitalization has revolutionized the way we perceive and implement security, introducing both new challenges and opportunities.

Cyber Threat Landscape:
The chapter also delves into the complex and dynamic landscape of cyber threats. From malicious hackers seeking financial gain to state-sponsored cyber espionage, the range and sophistication of threats continue to escalate. Understanding these threats is crucial for developing effective security strategies.

Data Protection and Privacy:

One of the central pillars of modern security is data protection and privacy. As individuals and organizations generate and exchange vast amounts of data, ensuring its confidentiality, integrity, and availability becomes paramount. We explore concepts such as encryption, access control, and data anonymization as key tools in safeguarding sensitive information.

Securing Critical Infrastructure:
Beyond digital data, the security of critical infrastructure such as power grids, transportation systems, and healthcare facilities is of utmost importance. We examine the interplay between physical and digital security measures, highlighting the need for comprehensive security frameworks.

Emerging Technologies and Challenges:
As technology evolves, so do the challenges and opportunities in security. Topics such as Internet of Things (IoT) security, artificial intelligence (AI) in cybersecurity, and quantum-resistant encryption are explored to provide insights into future security trends and considerations.

Human Factors in Security:
While technological solutions play a vital role, human behavior remains a significant factor in security vulnerabilities. From social engineering tactics to insider threats, understanding human psychology and promoting security awareness are essential aspects of a holistic security approach.

The Business Case for Security:
Finally, we examine the business implications of security investments. Beyond mitigating risks, effective security measures can enhance customer trust, regulatory compliance, and overall organizational resilience in the face of cyber threats.

By the end of this chapter, readers will gain a deeper appreciation for the multifaceted nature of security in today's digital age. Whether you are a cybersecurity professional, a business leader, or an individual concerned about personal privacy, understanding the fundamentals of security sets the stage for informed decision-making and proactive risk management in an increasingly interconnected world.

Chapter: Exploring Different Types of Security Threats

In the interconnected and digitized landscape of today, security threats come in various forms, each presenting unique challenges and risks to individuals, organizations, and societies at large. This chapter delves into the diverse array of security threats prevalent in the modern era, offering insights into their characteristics, impacts, and mitigation strategies.

1. Cyber Attacks:
Cyber attacks encompass a broad spectrum of malicious activities aimed at compromising digital systems, networks, or data. Common types of cyber attacks include:

Malware Attacks: Such as viruses, worms, Trojans, ransomware, and spyware, which infiltrate systems to steal data, disrupt operations, or extort money.

Phishing and Social Engineering: Deceptive techniques used to trick individuals into revealing sensitive information like passwords or financial details.

Denial-of-Service (DoS) and Distributed Denial-of-Service (DDoS) Attacks: Overwhelming systems or networks with traffic to disrupt services or render them inaccessible.

2. Insider Threats:

Insider threats arise from individuals within an organization who misuse their privileges or access to compromise security. This can include employees, contractors, or partners with malicious intent or inadvertently causing security breaches due to negligence.

3. Physical Security Threats:
Physical security threats target tangible assets such as buildings, equipment, and personnel. Examples include unauthorized access, theft, vandalism, and natural disasters like fires or floods that can disrupt operations and compromise safety.

4. Social Media Risks:
The widespread use of social media platforms introduces risks such as identity theft, reputational damage, exposure to scams or phishing attempts, and the inadvertent sharing of sensitive information.

5. Supply Chain Vulnerabilities:
Globalized supply chains are susceptible to disruptions and security breaches at various points, including suppliers, logistics, and distribution channels. Cyber attacks targeting supply chains can have cascading effects across industries and regions.

6. IoT (Internet of Things) Exploitation:
The proliferation of IoT devices introduces new security challenges due to their interconnected nature and often inadequate security measures. Compromised IoT devices can be exploited for data theft, network intrusions, or as entry points into larger systems.

7. Regulatory and Compliance Risks:

Failure to comply with industry regulations, data protection laws (such as GDPR or CCPA), or cybersecurity standards can expose organizations to legal penalties, financial losses, and reputational damage.

Mitigation Strategies:
Understanding these threats is the first step towards effective security management. Mitigation strategies include robust cybersecurity policies and protocols, employee training and awareness programs, access controls, encryption, intrusion detection systems, physical security measures, supply chain audits, and compliance frameworks.

By comprehensively addressing and proactively mitigating these diverse security threats, individuals and organizations can bolster their resilience, protect valuable assets, and safeguard against potential disruptions and harm in today's dynamic and interconnected environment.

Chapter: Security and Encryption

Fundamentals of Encryption and its Role in Data Security

In an age where digital data serves as the lifeblood of modern society, ensuring its confidentiality and integrity is paramount. Encryption stands as a fundamental pillar of cybersecurity, providing a robust mechanism for protecting sensitive information from unauthorized access and interception. This chapter delves into the core principles of encryption, its applications across various domains, and its indispensable role in safeguarding data security.

Understanding Encryption:
Encryption is the process of converting plaintext data into ciphertext using mathematical algorithms and cryptographic keys. This transformation renders the data unreadable to unauthorized entities, ensuring that only authorized parties with the corresponding decryption keys can access the original information.

Key Components of Encryption:

Cipher Algorithms: Encryption relies on sophisticated cipher algorithms such as Advanced Encryption Standard (AES), Rivest-Shamir-Adleman (RSA), and Data Encryption Standard (DES). These algorithms determine how data is transformed and secured.

Encryption Keys: Encryption keys are cryptographic codes used to encrypt and decrypt data. Symmetric encryption utilizes a single key for both encryption and decryption, while asymmetric encryption employs public and private key pairs.

Encryption in Data Transmission:
During data transmission over networks or the internet, encryption plays a crucial role in securing communications. Protocols like Transport Layer Security (TLS) and Secure Sockets Layer (SSL) leverage encryption to establish secure connections between clients and servers, protecting data from interception by malicious actors.

Data-at-Rest Encryption:
Encrypting data at rest — stored on devices, servers, or in databases — prevents unauthorized access in case of theft or unauthorized access attempts. Full disk encryption, file-level encryption, and database encryption are common techniques used to protect data at rest.

Role of Encryption in Data Security:

Confidentiality: Encryption ensures that only authorized users can access sensitive data, mitigating the risk of data breaches and unauthorized disclosures.

Integrity: By detecting unauthorized modifications to encrypted data (via cryptographic hashes or digital signatures), encryption helps maintain data integrity and trustworthiness.

Compliance: Many data protection regulations and standards, such as GDPR, HIPAA, and PCI DSS, mandate the use of encryption as part of data security and privacy measures.

Challenges and Considerations:

While encryption is a powerful tool, its effective implementation requires addressing key challenges such as key management, performance overhead, compatibility across systems, and ensuring encryption standards and protocols remain resilient against emerging threats.

Future Trends in Encryption:
Advancements in quantum computing and the evolution of encryption-resistant algorithms are shaping the future of encryption. Post-quantum cryptography, homomorphic encryption, and blockchain-based encryption are areas of ongoing research and development.

Conclusion:
Encryption stands as a cornerstone of modern data security strategies, offering a robust defense against unauthorized access and data breaches. Understanding encryption fundamentals equips individuals and organizations with the knowledge to implement effective encryption practices, protect sensitive data, and uphold the principles of confidentiality, integrity, and privacy in an increasingly interconnected world.

Chapter: Implementing Strong Encryption Practices

In the digital age, where data breaches and cyber threats loom large, implementing robust encryption practices is imperative for safeguarding sensitive information. This chapter delves into the key considerations and best practices for deploying strong encryption measures across various environments, ensuring data security and privacy.

Choosing Encryption Algorithms:
Selecting the right encryption algorithms is the first step towards strong data protection. Modern standards like AES (Advanced Encryption Standard) with key lengths of 256 bits offer high levels of security and are widely recommended for encrypting data at rest and in transit.

Key Management:
Effective key management is essential for encryption. Establishing policies and procedures for key generation, storage, distribution, rotation, and revocation ensures that encryption keys remain secure and accessible only to authorized entities. Consider using hardware security modules (HSMs) or key management services for added protection.

Utilizing Secure Protocols:
When transmitting sensitive data over networks or the internet, leverage secure communication protocols such as TLS (Transport Layer Security) or SSL (Secure Sockets Layer). These protocols encrypt data during transmission, protecting it from interception by malicious actors.

End-to-End Encryption (E2EE):
Implement end-to-end encryption mechanisms to secure data from sender to recipient without intermediaries being able to decipher the content. E2EE is crucial for messaging platforms, file sharing services, and any communication channels where privacy and confidentiality are paramount.

Secure Data Storage:
Encrypt data at rest using strong encryption methods such as AES for stored files, databases, and backups. Consider encrypting sensitive fields within databases or using file-level encryption for granular control over data protection.

Authentication and Access Control:
Combine encryption with robust authentication mechanisms such as multi-factor authentication (MFA) and access control policies. Ensure that only authorized users and applications have access to decrypted data based on their roles and permissions.

Regular Audits and Updates:
Conduct regular security audits and vulnerability assessments to identify encryption weaknesses or outdated algorithms. Stay abreast of encryption standards, industry best practices, and security patches to mitigate emerging threats effectively.

Compliance and Regulatory Requirements:
Align encryption practices with relevant regulatory frameworks such as GDPR, HIPAA, PCI DSS, or industry-specific standards. Encryption often plays a crucial role in meeting data protection and privacy compliance mandates.

Training and Awareness:

Educate employees, developers, and stakeholders about encryption principles, best practices, and the importance of data security. Foster a culture of security awareness and proactive risk mitigation across the organization.

Backup and Recovery Encryption:
Encrypt backup data to protect it from unauthorized access or tampering. Implement secure backup and recovery processes, including encryption keys management for disaster recovery scenarios.

Conclusion:
By implementing strong encryption practices across data storage, transmission, and access points, organizations can significantly enhance their cybersecurity posture and mitigate the risks associated with data breaches and cyber attacks. Encryption, when combined with robust key management, secure protocols, and compliance measures, forms a resilient defense mechanism to safeguard sensitive information in today's threat landscape.

Chapter: Privacy and Online Safety

Protecting Personal Data Online

In an era where digital interactions and transactions have become ubiquitous, safeguarding personal privacy, and ensuring online safety are paramount concerns. This chapter delves into the nuances of privacy protection and online safety practices, equipping individuals and organizations with the knowledge and strategies to navigate the digital landscape securely.

Understanding Privacy in the Digital Age:
Privacy encompasses the control individuals have over their personal information, including data collected, stored, and processed by various online platforms, services, and devices. As digital footprints expand, preserving privacy becomes increasingly complex yet essential.

Data Protection Principles:
Explore key data protection principles such as consent, purpose limitation, data minimization, accuracy, storage limitation, integrity, confidentiality, and accountability. Understanding these principles guides individuals and organizations in responsibly managing and protecting personal data.

Securing Online Accounts and Identities:

Implement robust password practices, including using strong, unique passwords for each account, enabling two-factor authentication (2FA), and regularly updating passwords. Educate users about phishing attacks, social engineering tactics, and the importance of vigilance in safeguarding account credentials.

Privacy Settings and Permissions:
Review and adjust privacy settings on social media platforms, apps, and online services to control data sharing, visibility of personal information, and targeted advertising. Understand how platforms collect, use, and share data to make informed privacy choices.

Data Encryption for Communication and Storage:
Utilize end-to-end encryption (E2EE) for messaging apps, email communications, and file sharing to protect sensitive information from unauthorized access during transit. Encrypt stored data on devices and cloud services using strong encryption standards to prevent data breaches.

Secure Browsing and Online Transactions:
Use secure HTTPS connections for browsing websites, especially when entering sensitive information such as login credentials, payment details, or personal data. Verify website security certificates and avoid unsecured public Wi-Fi networks for financial transactions or accessing sensitive accounts.

Privacy-Focused Tools and Technologies:
Explore privacy-enhancing tools such as virtual private networks (VPNs) for encrypted internet connections, ad blockers, tracking blockers, and privacy-focused browsers. Understand the benefits and limitations of these tools in enhancing online privacy.

Educational Awareness and Digital Literacy:
Promote digital literacy and privacy education initiatives to empower individuals, families, and communities with knowledge about online risks, privacy rights, and safe internet practices. Foster critical thinking skills to evaluate privacy policies, terms of service, and data sharing practices.

Regulatory Compliance and Privacy Laws:
Stay informed about data protection regulations such as GDPR, CCPA, and others applicable to your region or industry. Understand data subject rights, lawful data processing practices, breach notification requirements, and compliance obligations for organizations handling personal data.

Collaborative Privacy Advocacy:
Engage in privacy advocacy efforts, support privacy-conscious products and services, and participate in discussions about data ethics, transparency, and user rights. Advocate for stronger privacy regulations and accountability measures in the digital ecosystem.

Conclusion:
By prioritizing privacy protection and adopting proactive online safety measures, individuals and organizations can mitigate risks associated with data breaches, identity theft, online surveillance, and privacy violations. Empowering users with privacy knowledge, leveraging secure technologies, and fostering a culture of privacy awareness contribute to building a safer and more trustworthy digital environment for all stakeholders.

Chapter: Safeguarding Against Identity Theft and Fraud

Identity theft and fraud are pervasive threats in today's digital landscape, posing serious risks to individuals, businesses, and institutions. This chapter delves into the complexities of identity protection and fraud prevention, equipping readers with practical strategies and insights to mitigate these risks effectively.

Understanding Identity Theft and Fraud:
Identity theft involves unauthorized access to and misuse of personal information, such as Social Security numbers, credit card details, and passwords, for fraudulent purposes. Fraud encompasses a range of deceptive practices, including financial fraud, identity fraud, phishing scams, and social engineering tactics aimed at exploiting individuals or organizations.

Recognizing Common Threats and Techniques:
Explore common identity theft and fraud techniques, including phishing emails, fake websites, phone scams, pretexting, account takeover attacks, and identity spoofing. Understanding how these threats operate helps individuals and organizations identify and respond effectively to potential risks.

Strengthening Password Security:

Implement strong password practices, including using complex passwords or passphrases, avoiding password reuse across accounts, and regularly updating passwords. Consider using password managers to securely store and manage credentials across different platforms.

Two-Factor Authentication (2FA) and Multi-Factor Authentication (MFA):
Enable 2FA or MFA wherever possible to add an extra layer of security to online accounts and systems. Authentication codes sent to mobile devices or generated by authentication apps provide additional verification beyond passwords, reducing the risk of unauthorized access.

Monitoring Financial Accounts and Credit Reports:
Regularly monitor bank statements, credit card transactions, and credit reports for any unauthorized or suspicious activities. Promptly report discrepancies or fraudulent transactions to financial institutions and credit bureaus for investigation and resolution.

Secure Online Shopping and Transactions:
Exercise caution when shopping online, especially on unfamiliar websites. Look for secure HTTPS connections, use reputable payment gateways, and avoid sharing sensitive information over unsecured networks or email communications.

Data Privacy and Sharing Awareness:
Be cautious about sharing personal information online or over the phone, especially in response to unsolicited requests or suspicious messages. Verify the legitimacy of requests and the identity of individuals or organizations before disclosing sensitive data.

Educating Against Social Engineering Tactics:

Educate yourself and your employees about social engineering tactics such as phishing, pretexting, and baiting. Recognize red flags such as urgent requests for sensitive information, unusual payment requests, or unsolicited offers that seem too good to be true.

Securing Devices and Networks:
Keep software, operating systems, and antivirus programs updated on devices to mitigate vulnerabilities exploited by cybercriminals. Use secure Wi-Fi networks, firewalls, and encryption protocols for data transmission and communications.

Reporting and Responding to Identity Theft or Fraud:
Act promptly if you suspect identity theft or fraudulent activities. Contact relevant financial institutions, credit bureaus, and law enforcement agencies to report incidents, freeze accounts, and initiate investigations or legal actions, as necessary.

Collaborative Awareness and Prevention Efforts:
Engage in community or industry initiatives focused on identity theft prevention, cybersecurity awareness, and fraud detection. Share best practices, resources, and insights to collectively strengthen defenses against identity-related crimes.

Conclusion:
By adopting proactive measures such as strong authentication, vigilant monitoring, privacy-conscious behaviors, and ongoing education, individuals and organizations can significantly reduce the risk of falling victim to identity theft and fraud. Collaboration, awareness, and a proactive approach to cybersecurity are key in safeguarding identities and financial assets in today's digital environment.

Chapter: Hacking Demystified

Understanding Hackers and Their Motivations

Hacking is a term that often conjures images of nefarious individuals exploiting vulnerabilities for malicious purposes. However, the reality is more nuanced, with hackers spanning a spectrum of motivations, skills, and ethical considerations. This chapter dives into the world of hacking, demystifying common misconceptions and shedding light on the diverse motivations driving individuals in this realm.

The Hacker Spectrum:
Hackers are often categorized based on their intentions and ethical considerations:

White Hat Hackers: Ethical hackers who use their skills to identify and mitigate security vulnerabilities, often employed by organizations for penetration testing and security assessments.
Black Hat Hackers: Malicious hackers who exploit vulnerabilities for personal gain, financial motives, espionage, or causing harm.
Grey Hat Hackers: Individuals who operate between ethical and unethical boundaries, sometimes exposing vulnerabilities without authorization but with no malicious intent.
Motivations Behind Hacking:

Understanding hacker motivations is crucial for comprehending their actions and potential impacts. Motivations can vary widely and may include:

Financial Gain: Cybercriminals engage in hacking for monetary benefits, such as stealing financial information, ransomware attacks, or selling stolen data on the dark web.

Political or Ideological Motives: Hacktivists target organizations or entities to promote political ideologies, social causes, or protest actions.

Espionage and State-Sponsored Hacking: Nation-states and intelligence agencies conduct cyber espionage, gather intelligence, or disrupt rival nations' infrastructure for strategic advantages.

Challenge and Curiosity: Some hackers are driven by intellectual curiosity, technical challenges, or the desire to explore and understand complex systems.

Revenge or Malicious Intent: Individuals may engage in hacking out of revenge, vendettas, or malicious intent aimed at causing harm or embarrassment to specific targets.

Common Hacking Techniques and Tools:

Hackers employ a range of techniques and tools to exploit vulnerabilities and gain unauthorized access:

Social Engineering: Manipulating individuals or employees through psychological tactics to divulge sensitive information or perform actions that compromise security.

Phishing and Spear Phishing: Sending deceptive emails or messages to trick recipients into clicking malicious links, downloading malware, or revealing credentials.

Exploiting Software Vulnerabilities: Leveraging weaknesses in software, applications, or systems to gain unauthorized access, execute code, or escalate privileges.

Brute Force Attacks: Systematically trying all possible combinations of passwords or keys to gain access to accounts or systems.

Malware: Deploying malicious software such as viruses, worms, Trojans, ransomware, or spyware to compromise systems, steal data, or disrupt operations.

Ethical Considerations and Legal Implications:
Ethical hackers adhere to principles of responsible disclosure, obtaining proper authorization before testing systems, and adhering to legal and ethical guidelines. Unethical hacking can lead to severe legal consequences, including fines, imprisonment, and damage to reputations.

Mitigating Hacking Risks:
Organizations and individuals can mitigate hacking risks by implementing robust cybersecurity measures, including:

Conducting regular security assessments, vulnerability scans, and penetration testing.
Educating employees and users about cybersecurity best practices, phishing awareness, and password hygiene.
Deploying firewalls, intrusion detection systems (IDS), antivirus software, and encryption protocols.
Monitoring network traffic, logging security events, and implementing access controls and least privilege principles.
Keeping software, operating systems, and firmware updated with security patches and fixes.

Conclusion:

By demystifying hacking and understanding the diverse motivations behind hacker activities, individuals and organizations can adopt proactive cybersecurity strategies, enhance resilience against cyber threats, and foster a culture of ethical and responsible digital conduct. Collaboration between security professionals, ethical hackers, law enforcement agencies, and regulatory bodies plays a crucial role in mitigating hacking risks and safeguarding digital ecosystems.

Chapter: Techniques and Tools Used in Ethical Hacking

Ethical hacking, also known as penetration testing or white-hat hacking, plays a crucial role in identifying and mitigating security vulnerabilities before malicious actors exploit them. This chapter explores the techniques, methodologies, and tools employed by ethical hackers to assess and strengthen the security posture of systems, networks, and applications.

Understanding Ethical Hacking:
Ethical hacking involves authorized attempts to simulate cyber attacks and security breaches to uncover weaknesses in systems, networks, or applications. Ethical hackers, often employed by organizations or security firms, use their skills and knowledge to proactively identify and remediate vulnerabilities, thereby enhancing overall cybersecurity.

Reconnaissance and Information Gathering:
Ethical hackers begin by gathering information about the target environment, including IP addresses, domain names, network topology, system configurations, and publicly available information about the organization. Techniques such as passive reconnaissance (e.g., search engines, social media) and active reconnaissance (e.g., network scanning, port scanning) provide valuable insights.

Vulnerability Scanning and Assessment:

Using automated scanning tools such as Nessus, OpenVAS, or Qualys, ethical hackers conduct vulnerability assessments to identify known vulnerabilities in systems, services, and applications. Vulnerability scanners detect issues such as outdated software, misconfigurations, missing patches, and common security weaknesses.

Exploitation and Penetration Testing:
Ethical hackers leverage identified vulnerabilities to simulate real-world attacks and gain unauthorized access to systems or sensitive data. Techniques such as exploitation of software flaws (e.g., buffer overflow, SQL injection, cross-site scripting) and privilege escalation are used to demonstrate potential risks and impacts.

Password Cracking and Authentication Testing:
Testing the strength of passwords and authentication mechanisms is crucial in assessing security resilience. Ethical hackers use tools like John the Ripper, Hashcat, or Hydra to crack passwords, perform brute-force attacks, or test weak authentication protocols (e.g., insecure protocols like FTP, Telnet).

Wireless Network Auditing:
Assessing the security of wireless networks (Wi-Fi) is essential to prevent unauthorized access and data interception. Ethical hackers use tools such as Aircrack-ng, Kismet, or Wireshark to analyze wireless traffic, detect rogue access points, and test encryption strength (e.g., WEP, WPA, WPA2, WPA3).

Social Engineering Simulations:

Ethical hackers conduct social engineering tests to evaluate human vulnerabilities within organizations. Phishing simulations, pretexting calls, physical security assessments (e.g., tailgating), and USB drop attacks are examples of techniques used to assess employee awareness and adherence to security policies.

Reporting and Remediation:
After conducting ethical hacking tests, detailed reports outlining vulnerabilities, exploit paths, risk levels, and recommendations for remediation are provided to stakeholders. Collaborative discussions and prioritization of security fixes and patches are essential for strengthening defenses.

Continuous Monitoring and Red Teaming:
Ethical hacking is an ongoing process, and organizations benefit from continuous monitoring, threat intelligence analysis, and red teaming exercises. Red teams simulate sophisticated cyber attacks to test incident response capabilities, detection mechanisms, and resilience under pressure.

Legal and Ethical Considerations:
Ethical hackers must operate within legal and ethical boundaries, obtaining proper authorization, respecting privacy laws, and adhering to responsible disclosure principles. Non-disclosure agreements (NDAs), ethical hacking certifications (e.g., CEH, OSCP), and adherence to industry standards (e.g., ISO 27001) contribute to ethical hacking practices.

Conclusion:

Ethical hacking is a proactive and essential component of cybersecurity strategies, enabling organizations to identify and address vulnerabilities before they are exploited by malicious actors. By employing a combination of reconnaissance, vulnerability assessment, exploitation, social engineering tests, and continuous monitoring, ethical hackers play a vital role in enhancing digital resilience and fostering a security-aware culture within organizations. Collaboration between ethical hackers, security teams, and stakeholders ensures robust defenses against evolving cyber threats.

Chapter: Networking and Cloud Computing Security

Securing Networks Against Cyber Attacks

Networking and cloud computing are foundational pillars of modern digital infrastructure, enabling seamless communication, collaboration, and data access. However, their widespread adoption also presents significant security challenges. This chapter delves into the key principles, strategies, and technologies essential for securing networks and cloud environments against cyber attacks.

Understanding Networking Security:
Networking security encompasses measures and protocols designed to protect the integrity, confidentiality, and availability of data transmitted over networks. It involves securing network devices, data transmissions, access controls, and monitoring for suspicious activities.

Network Segmentation and Access Controls:

Implementing network segmentation divides networks into distinct segments or zones, reducing the impact of potential breaches, and limiting lateral movement by attackers. Coupled with robust access controls, such as firewalls, virtual private networks (VPNs), and role-based access control (RBAC), organizations can enforce least privilege principles and mitigate unauthorized access risks.

Encryption for Network Traffic:
Encrypting network traffic using protocols like TLS/SSL (Transport Layer Security/Secure Sockets Layer) ensures data confidentiality and integrity during transmission over insecure networks or public channels. VPNs provide encrypted tunnels for secure remote access and inter-site communications, safeguarding sensitive information from eavesdropping or interception.

Intrusion Detection and Prevention Systems (IDPS):
Deploying IDPS solutions helps detect and respond to suspicious activities, anomalous traffic patterns, and potential cyber threats in real-time. IDPS solutions can be signature-based (detect known threats) or behavior-based (identify abnormal activities), enhancing network security posture and incident response capabilities.

Network Monitoring and Logging:
Comprehensive network monitoring tools and logging mechanisms capture and analyze network traffic, system logs, and security events. Monitoring for anomalies, unauthorized access attempts, malware activity, or configuration changes enables proactive threat detection, forensic analysis, and compliance auditing.

Cloud Computing Security Considerations:

Cloud environments offer scalability, flexibility, and cost-efficiency but require robust security measures due to shared responsibility models and potential exposure to new threats. Key considerations include:

Identity and Access Management (IAM): Implement strong authentication, least privilege access controls, and centralized IAM policies to manage user identities, permissions, and credentials across cloud services.

Data Encryption and Privacy: Encrypt data at rest and in transit within cloud environments using strong encryption standards. Ensure compliance with data protection regulations (e.g., GDPR, CCPA) and data residency requirements.

Cloud Security Services: Leverage cloud-native security services such as AWS Security Hub, Azure Security Center, and Google Cloud Security Command Center for continuous monitoring, threat detection, and compliance management.

Secure Configuration and Patch Management: Regularly update and patch cloud resources, virtual machines, containers, and APIs to address vulnerabilities and reduce attack surfaces. Follow secure configuration guidelines provided by cloud service providers (CSPs) and industry standards.

Backup and Disaster Recovery: Implement data backup strategies, disaster recovery plans, and business continuity measures to mitigate data loss, downtime, and service disruptions in cloud environments.

Collaboration with CSPs and Security Partners: Engage with CSPs, cloud security providers, and cybersecurity experts to leverage industry best practices, threat intelligence, and security tools tailored to cloud environments. Collaborate on incident response planning, shared responsibility models, and security assessments to strengthen cloud security posture.

Educating Cloud Users and Administrators:
Provide training, awareness programs, and guidelines for cloud users, developers, and administrators on secure cloud practices, data handling policies, and incident response procedures. Foster a culture of security awareness, accountability, and continuous learning within cloud teams.

Compliance and Audit Readiness:
Align cloud security practices with regulatory requirements, industry standards (e.g., CSA, NIST), and CSP-specific security frameworks (e.g., AWS Well-Architected Framework, Azure Security Benchmark). Conduct regular security assessments, audits, and penetration testing exercises to validate security controls and ensure compliance.

Conclusion:
Securing networks and cloud environments requires a multi-layered approach encompassing network segmentation, access controls, encryption, monitoring, cloud-native security services, and collaborative partnerships with CSPs and security experts. By prioritizing cybersecurity hygiene, adopting best practices, and staying vigilant against evolving threats, organizations can enhance network resilience, protect sensitive data, and maintain trust in their digital operations within cloud ecosystems.

Chapter: Best Practices for Cloud Security

Cloud computing offers unprecedented scalability, agility, and cost-efficiency, revolutionizing how organizations manage and deliver IT services. However, the shared responsibility model inherent in cloud environments necessitates robust security measures to protect data, applications, and infrastructure. This chapter explores essential best practices for ensuring cloud security across various deployment models (public, private, hybrid) and service models (IaaS, PaaS, SaaS).

Understanding the Shared Responsibility Model: Cloud providers adhere to a shared responsibility model where they secure the underlying infrastructure (physical servers, networking, data centers), while customers are responsible for securing their data, applications, identities, configurations, and access controls within the cloud environment.

1. Identity and Access Management (IAM):

Implement strong authentication mechanisms such as multi-factor authentication (MFA), single sign-on (SSO), and role-based access controls (RBAC) to manage user identities and permissions effectively. Regularly review and revoke unnecessary privileges to minimize attack surfaces.

2. Data Encryption:
Encrypt data at rest and in transit using robust encryption standards (e.g., AES-256 for data-at-rest, TLS/SSL for data in transit). Leverage cloud-native encryption services (e.g., AWS KMS, Azure Key Vault) for managing encryption keys securely and implementing data encryption policies.

3. Secure Configurations and Patch Management:
Follow secure configuration guidelines provided by cloud service providers (CSPs) for virtual machines, containers, databases, and networking components. Apply security patches and updates promptly to mitigate vulnerabilities and protect against known exploits.

4. Network Security Controls:
Implement network segmentation, firewalls, virtual private networks (VPNs), and intrusion detection/prevention systems (IDPS) to monitor and control network traffic within cloud environments. Use security groups, network ACLs, and routing controls to enforce least privilege access and protect against unauthorized access attempts.

5. Logging, Monitoring, and Auditing:
Enable logging and monitoring for cloud resources, applications, and user activities to detect anomalies, security incidents, and compliance deviations. Use cloud-native monitoring tools (e.g., AWS CloudWatch, Azure Monitor, Google Cloud Monitoring) and security information and event management (SIEM) solutions for centralized log management and real-time threat detection.

6. Data Backup and Recovery:
Implement automated backup policies and disaster recovery plans for critical data and applications in cloud environments. Test backup restoration processes regularly to ensure data integrity, availability, and business continuity in case of disruptions or data loss incidents.

7. Cloud Security Governance and Compliance:
Establish cloud security policies, standards, and procedures aligned with industry regulations (e.g., GDPR, HIPAA, PCI DSS) and compliance frameworks. Conduct regular security assessments, audits, and penetration testing exercises to validate security controls, identify gaps, and address vulnerabilities.

8. Cloud Security Training and Awareness:
Provide comprehensive security training and awareness programs for cloud users, developers, administrators, and stakeholders. Educate teams on secure cloud practices, data classification, incident response procedures, and emerging threats to foster a culture of security and accountability.

9. Incident Response and Cloud Forensics:
Develop and maintain incident response plans tailored to cloud environments, including predefined roles, communication channels, escalation procedures, and forensic investigation protocols. Collaborate with CSPs, incident response teams, and legal experts to mitigate and respond effectively to security incidents, breaches, or data breaches.

10. Continuous Improvement and Adaptation:

Embrace a continuous improvement mindset for cloud security, regularly reviewing and updating security policies, controls, and response plans based on evolving threats, industry trends, and lessons learned from security incidents. Stay informed about cloud security best practices, emerging technologies, and CSP security features to adapt and optimize security postures.

Conclusion:
Effective cloud security requires a holistic approach encompassing identity management, encryption, secure configurations, network controls, monitoring, compliance, training, incident response, and ongoing optimization. By implementing best practices, leveraging cloud-native security tools, collaborating with CSPs, and fostering a security-conscious culture, organizations can mitigate risks, protect sensitive data, and build resilient cloud infrastructures capable of supporting digital transformation initiatives securely.

Chapter: Certification for Security Professionals

Overview of Industry-Recognized Security Certifications

In the rapidly evolving field of cybersecurity, obtaining industry-recognized certifications is crucial for security professionals to demonstrate their knowledge, skills, and expertise in various domains of information security. This chapter provides an overview of prominent security certifications, their significance, and the career benefits they offer to individuals pursuing roles in cybersecurity and information assurance.

1. Certified Information Systems Security Professional (CISSP):
CISSP is a globally recognized certification offered by (ISC)², focusing on cybersecurity leadership and expertise across eight domains, including security and risk management, asset security, security architecture, and engineering. CISSP certification validates professionals' ability to design, implement, and manage cybersecurity programs effectively.

2. Certified Ethical Hacker (CEH):

CEH, provided by EC-Council, is designed for ethical hackers, penetration testers, and security professionals focusing on offensive security techniques. CEH certification validates skills in identifying vulnerabilities, performing ethical hacking assessments, and understanding countermeasures to protect systems and networks.

3. CompTIA Security+:
Security+ is an entry-level certification by CompTIA, ideal for beginners or professionals seeking foundational knowledge in cybersecurity concepts, risk management, network security, cryptography, and incident response. Security+ certification is vendor-neutral and serves as a stepping stone to advanced cybersecurity roles.

4. Certified Information Security Manager (CISM):
CISM, offered by ISACA, targets information security managers and professionals responsible for managing, designing, and overseeing information security programs within organizations. CISM certification validates skills in risk management, governance, incident response, and information security strategy.

5. Certified Information Systems Auditor (CISA):
CISA, also provided by ISACA, focuses on auditing, control, and assurance skills for information systems professionals. CISA certification validates expertise in auditing processes, IT governance, risk management, and information system controls, essential for ensuring compliance and security.

6. Offensive Security Certified Professional (OSCP):

OSCP, offered by Offensive Security, is a hands-on and practical certification focusing on penetration testing and ethical hacking skills. OSCP certification requires passing a challenging 24-hour hands-on exam, demonstrating proficiency in real-world penetration testing scenarios and techniques.

7. Certified Cloud Security Professional (CCSP):
CCSP, offered by (ISC)², targets professionals involved in cloud security architecture, design, operations, and governance. CCSP certification validates expertise in cloud security concepts, cloud architecture, data security, compliance, and risk management within cloud environments.

8. Cisco Certified CyberOps Associate:
This certification, offered by Cisco, focuses on cybersecurity operations skills, including security monitoring, incident response, threat intelligence, and automation. CyberOps Associate certification validates skills in detecting and mitigating cybersecurity threats within networked environments.

9. Certified Information Privacy Professional (CIPP):
CIPP certifications, offered by the International Association of Privacy Professionals (IAPP), validate expertise in data privacy laws, regulations, compliance frameworks, and privacy management practices. CIPP certifications cover various domains, including privacy program governance, data protection assessments, and privacy technology.

10. GIAC Security Essentials (GSEC):

GSEC, provided by GIAC (Global Information Assurance Certification), is an entry-level certification focusing on general information security concepts, principles, tools, and techniques. GSEC certification validates skills in network security, cryptography, incident handling, and security policies.

Choosing the Right Certification Path:
Selecting the appropriate certification depends on individual career goals, current job roles, experience levels, and areas of interest within cybersecurity. Consider factors such as certification prerequisites, exam formats, renewal requirements, industry recognition, and alignment with career aspirations and job roles.

Benefits of Security Certifications:

Validation of Skills: Certifications validate expertise, skills, and knowledge in specific cybersecurity domains, enhancing credibility and marketability for professionals.
Career Advancement: Certified professionals often enjoy expanded job opportunities, promotions, salary enhancements, and recognition within their organizations and the cybersecurity industry.
Industry Recognition: Employers value industry-recognized certifications as indicators of professionals' commitment to ongoing learning, best practices, and maintaining high standards of security excellence.
Professional Networking: Certification programs often include membership in professional organizations, forums, and networking opportunities, facilitating collaboration, knowledge sharing, and career growth within the cybersecurity community.

Conclusion:

Security certifications play a pivotal role in validating cybersecurity skills, advancing careers, and meeting industry demands for qualified professionals capable of addressing evolving cyber threats and challenges. Choosing the right certification path, maintaining continuous learning, gaining hands-on experience, and leveraging professional networks contribute to successful cybersecurity careers and organizational security resilience in today's dynamic threat landscape.

Chapter: Advancing Your Career in the Security Field

The field of cybersecurity and information security offers dynamic and rewarding career opportunities for professionals with a passion for protecting digital assets, mitigating risks, and staying ahead of evolving cyber threats. This chapter explores strategies, skills, certifications, and career pathways for individuals looking to advance and excel in the security domain.

1. Continuous Learning and Skill Development: Cybersecurity is a rapidly evolving field, requiring professionals to stay updated with the latest trends, technologies, threats, and mitigation strategies. Engage in continuous learning through formal education, industry certifications, online courses, workshops, conferences, and networking events.

2. Specialization and Domain Expertise:

Identify areas of specialization within cybersecurity that align with your interests, strengths, and career goals. Specializations may include network security, cloud security, penetration testing, incident response, governance, risk management, compliance, cryptography, or threat intelligence.

3. Pursuing Industry-Recognized Certifications:
Earn industry-recognized certifications such as CISSP, CEH, CISM, Security+, CCSP, or specialized certifications relevant to your career path. Certifications validate skills, enhance credibility, open doors to new opportunities, and demonstrate commitment to excellence in cybersecurity.

4. Gaining Hands-On Experience:
Gain practical experience through internships, entry-level roles, volunteer work, cybersecurity competitions (e.g., Capture The Flag events), or contributing to open-source security projects. Hands-on experience complements theoretical knowledge, hones technical skills, and prepares you for real-world challenges.

5. Building a Professional Network:
Network with cybersecurity professionals, industry experts, mentors, and peers through professional organizations, forums, social media platforms (e.g., LinkedIn, Twitter), and local cybersecurity meetups or chapters. Networking fosters collaborations, knowledge sharing, career insights, and mentorship opportunities.

6. Developing Soft Skills:

In addition to technical expertise, cultivate essential soft skills such as communication, problem-solving, critical thinking, teamwork, leadership, and adaptability. Effective communication skills are particularly valuable for conveying complex security concepts, collaborating with diverse teams, and influencing decision-makers.

7. Contributing to Cybersecurity Communities:
Contribute to cybersecurity communities, forums, blogs, or social media groups by sharing insights, participating in discussions, presenting at conferences, or publishing research papers. Active involvement in the cybersecurity community enhances visibility, builds reputation, and expands professional networks.

8. Seeking Advanced Education and Training:
Consider pursuing advanced degrees (e.g., Master's in Cybersecurity, Information Assurance, Computer Science) or specialized training programs to deepen expertise, gain managerial skills, and qualify for senior-level roles such as cybersecurity manager, architect, consultant, or CISO (Chief Information Security Officer).

9. Exploring Career Pathways:
Explore diverse career pathways within cybersecurity, including roles such as security analyst, penetration tester, security engineer, incident responder, security architect, compliance officer, threat intelligence analyst, cybersecurity consultant, or risk manager. Tailor your career path based on interests, strengths, and industry demands.

10. Stay Ethical, Adhere to Ethics and Standards:

Maintain ethical conduct, integrity, and respect for privacy, laws, regulations, and industry standards (e.g., GDPR, HIPAA, PCI DSS) in all security activities. Upholding ethical principles enhances trust, credibility, and long-term success in the security profession.

11. Setting Career Goals and Seeking Mentorship:
Set clear career goals, create a career development plan, and seek mentorship from experienced cybersecurity professionals or industry leaders. Mentors provide guidance, advice, insights, and support in navigating career challenges, seizing opportunities, and achieving career milestones.

Conclusion:
Advancing in the security field requires a combination of technical skills, continuous learning, certifications, hands-on experience, networking, soft skills, ethical conduct, career planning, and mentorship. Embrace lifelong learning, adaptability, and a proactive mindset to thrive in the dynamic and ever-evolving landscape of cybersecurity, contributing to organizational security resilience and shaping the future of cybersecurity excellence.

Chapter: Viruses and Malware

Identifying and Preventing Common Malicious Software

Viruses and malware represent persistent threats to digital security, capable of causing data breaches, system disruptions, financial losses, and privacy violations. This chapter delves into the various types of malicious software, their behaviors, propagation methods, and effective prevention strategies to safeguard systems, networks, and data against cyber threats.

Understanding Malicious Software:
Malicious software, commonly known as malware, encompasses a wide range of malicious programs designed to infiltrate, damage, or control computer systems, devices, and networks without authorization. Malware includes viruses, worms, Trojans, ransomware, spyware, adware, rootkits, and more, each with distinct functionalities and impacts.

1. Viruses:

Viruses are self-replicating programs that attach themselves to legitimate files or programs, spreading across systems when infected files are executed. Viruses can corrupt data, delete files, steal information, or create backdoors for remote attackers.

2. Worms:
Worms are standalone programs that replicate and spread across networks independently, exploiting vulnerabilities in network protocols or software. Worms often consume network bandwidth, propagate rapidly, and may carry payloads for malicious activities like data theft or system exploitation.

3. Trojans (Trojan Horses):
Trojans disguise themselves as legitimate software or files to deceive users into downloading and executing them. Once activated, Trojans can perform unauthorized actions such as stealing sensitive data, granting remote access, launching denial-of-service (DoS) attacks, or installing additional malware.

4. Ransomware:
Ransomware encrypts files or locks users out of their systems, demanding payment (usually in cryptocurrency) for decryption keys or restoration of access. Ransomware attacks can cripple businesses, disrupt operations, and lead to significant financial losses and data breaches.

5. Spyware and Adware:
Spyware covertly monitors user activities, collects sensitive information (e.g., keystrokes, browsing habits, login credentials), and reports data to malicious actors. Adware, while less malicious, displays unwanted advertisements, alters browser settings, and may degrade system performance.

Identifying Signs of Infection:
Recognizing symptoms of malware infections is crucial for early detection and containment. Common signs include unusual system behavior (e.g., slow performance, crashes), unauthorized file modifications, unexpected pop-up ads, unusual network traffic, and security software alerts.

Preventive Measures Against Malware:
Implementing robust cybersecurity practices and tools can significantly reduce the risk of malware infections and mitigate their impacts:

Antivirus/Anti-Malware Software: Install reputable antivirus/anti-malware solutions on all devices, ensuring regular updates and scheduled scans to detect and remove malicious software.

Firewalls and Intrusion Prevention Systems (IPS): Configure firewalls and IPS solutions to monitor and block unauthorized network traffic, malicious connections, and known attack patterns.

Secure Email and Web Browsing: Educate users about phishing scams, malicious email attachments, and suspicious website links. Use email filtering, web content filtering, and secure browsing practices (HTTPS, avoiding untrusted sites) to mitigate risks.

Patch and Update Management: Keep operating systems, applications, firmware, and security software updated with the latest patches and security updates to address known vulnerabilities exploited by malware.

User Education and Awareness: Conduct cybersecurity training programs for employees, emphasizing safe computing practices, password hygiene, avoiding unauthorized downloads, and reporting suspicious activities promptly.

Data Backup and Recovery: Regularly back up critical data to secure offline or cloud storage, ensuring data integrity and availability in case of ransomware attacks or data loss incidents. Test backup restoration procedures periodically.

Access Controls and Least Privilege: Implement least privilege principles, role-based access controls (RBAC), and strong authentication mechanisms (e.g., MFA) to limit user privileges, restrict access to sensitive data/systems, and prevent unauthorized activities by malware.

Incident Response and Recovery Plans: Develop and practice incident response plans, including malware containment, investigation, mitigation, data recovery, and communication protocols. Establish clear roles, responsibilities, and escalation procedures for responding to malware incidents effectively.

Conclusion:

Combatting viruses and malware requires a multi-layered approach combining proactive prevention, user education, threat detection, and incident response readiness. By staying vigilant, implementing security best practices, leveraging technology safeguards, and fostering a security-aware culture, organizations can reduce their exposure to malware threats and protect their digital assets from harm. Regular risk assessments, security audits, and collaboration with cybersecurity experts further enhance resilience against evolving malware threats in today's interconnected digital landscape.

Chapter: Steps to Take in Case of a Malware Attack

Facing a malware attack can be a stressful and critical situation for individuals and organizations. Responding promptly and effectively is crucial to mitigate damages, restore systems, and safeguard data integrity. This chapter outlines essential steps to take in case of a malware attack, guiding individuals and security teams through the incident response process.

1. Recognize Indicators of a Malware Attack:
Be vigilant for signs indicating a malware infection such as unusual system behavior (slowdowns, crashes), unexpected pop-up messages, unauthorized file modifications, suspicious network activity, or antivirus alerts.

2. Isolate Infected Systems:
Immediately disconnect or isolate infected systems from the network (physically or logically) to prevent further spread of malware to other devices or servers. Disable wireless connections and disconnect network cables, as necessary.

3. Alert Relevant Parties:
Notify IT/security teams, management, and relevant stakeholders about the malware incident. Ensure clear communication channels and escalation procedures are in place to coordinate response efforts effectively.

4. Gather Information and Assess Impact:
Collect information about the malware symptoms, affected systems, potential entry points, and any recent suspicious activities. Assess the impact on data integrity, system availability, critical services, and business operations.

5. Activate Incident Response Plan:
Follow established incident response procedures outlined in the organization's incident response plan (IRP). Assign roles and responsibilities to team members for malware analysis, containment, eradication, recovery, and communication.

6. Malware Analysis and Identification:
Perform malware analysis (if feasible) or engage cybersecurity experts to identify the type, behavior, and capabilities of the malware. Determine how the malware entered the system (e.g., phishing emails, malicious downloads, unpatched vulnerabilities).

7. Contain and Remediate Infected Systems:
Contain the malware by isolating infected systems further, disabling affected services, or implementing network segmentation. Use updated antivirus/anti-malware tools to scan and remove malicious files, processes, and registry entries from compromised systems.

8. Restore Data and Systems:

Restore affected data and systems from clean backups stored in secure locations. Verify backup integrity and completeness before restoration. Reimage or rebuild compromised systems if necessary to ensure malware eradication.

9. Implement Security Improvements:
Identify security gaps, vulnerabilities, or weaknesses exploited by the malware attack. Implement security patches, updates, and configuration changes to strengthen defenses and prevent future infections. Review access controls, policies, and security configurations for compliance and best practices.

10. Monitor and Learn from the Incident:
Monitor systems, logs, and network traffic for post-incident activities, residual malware traces, or potential reinfections. Conduct post-incident reviews (post-mortems) to analyze response effectiveness, lessons learned, and recommendations for enhancing incident response capabilities and security posture.

11. Educate and Train Users:
Provide cybersecurity awareness training to employees, emphasizing malware prevention techniques, safe browsing habits, phishing awareness, and reporting procedures for suspicious activities. Encourage a security-conscious culture across the organization.

12. Engage External Support if Needed:
In complex or severe malware incidents, consider engaging external cybersecurity firms, incident response teams, or law enforcement agencies (if applicable) for forensic analysis, threat intelligence, legal guidance, and regulatory compliance.

Conclusion:

Being prepared to respond to a malware attack is as crucial as preventing one. By following structured incident response procedures, leveraging technical tools, engaging cybersecurity expertise, and fostering a culture of security awareness, organizations can effectively mitigate the impact of malware incidents, minimize downtime, protect data assets, and strengthen overall cybersecurity resilience. Regular incident simulations, drills, and continuous improvement in security practices further enhance readiness and response effectiveness in the face of evolving cyber threats.

Chapter: Food Safety and Security

Importance of Food Safety Regulations

Ensuring food safety is paramount in safeguarding public health, maintaining consumer trust, and upholding quality standards in the food industry. This chapter delves into the significance of food safety regulations, the complexities of foodborne hazards, and strategies for enhancing food safety and security across the supply chain.

1. Understanding Food Safety Hazards:

Food safety hazards encompass biological, chemical, and physical contaminants that can compromise the safety and quality of food products. Common hazards include bacteria (e.g., Salmonella, E. coli), viruses, parasites, allergens, chemical toxins (e.g., pesticides, additives), foreign objects, and cross-contamination risks.

2. Impact of Foodborne Illnesses:
Foodborne illnesses resulting from contaminated food can lead to a range of health issues from mild gastroenteritis to severe infections, organ damage, and even fatalities, particularly affecting vulnerable populations such as children, elderly individuals, pregnant women, and immunocompromised individuals.

3. Role of Food Safety Regulations:
Food safety regulations, enforced by government agencies (e.g., FDA in the U.S., EFSA in Europe), set standards, guidelines, and inspection protocols to ensure food safety throughout the production, processing, distribution, and consumption stages. Regulations cover hygiene practices, sanitation, labeling, packaging, temperature control, allergen management, and hazard analysis (HACCP).

4. Compliance with Good Manufacturing Practices (GMPs):
Adhering to Good Manufacturing Practices is essential for food producers, processors, and handlers to maintain hygienic conditions, prevent contamination, and meet regulatory requirements. GMPs cover facility cleanliness, personnel hygiene, equipment maintenance, pest control, and documentation of processes.

5. Hazard Analysis and Critical Control Points (HACCP):

HACCP is a systematic approach to food safety management that identifies, evaluates, and controls hazards at critical stages of food production and handling. HACCP plans include hazard analysis, critical control point identification, monitoring procedures, corrective actions, verification, and record-keeping.

6. Allergen Management and Labeling:
Proper allergen management is crucial to prevent allergic reactions in sensitive individuals. Food manufacturers must accurately label allergens (e.g., peanuts, gluten, milk) on product packaging, implement segregation measures, train staff, and ensure thorough cleaning to prevent cross-contact.

7. Food Defense and Security Measures:
Beyond food safety, food defense focuses on protecting the food supply chain from intentional contamination, sabotage, or terrorism threats. Implementing food defense plans, conducting vulnerability assessments, enhancing access controls, and training employees on security protocols are vital aspects.

8. Supply Chain Traceability and Transparency:
Enhanced traceability using technologies such as blockchain, RFID tags, and supply chain management systems enables rapid identification and recall of contaminated food products, reducing public health risks and preserving consumer confidence in food safety.

9. Training and Education Programs:
Continuous training and education for food handlers, managers, and stakeholders on food safety principles, regulations, hygiene practices, sanitation protocols, and emergency response procedures are crucial for maintaining compliance and fostering a culture of food safety awareness.

10. Collaboration and Industry Standards:
Collaboration among food industry stakeholders, regulators, academia, and consumer advocacy groups fosters information sharing, best practices adoption, research collaboration, and development of industry standards (e.g., ISO 22000) to improve food safety and security globally.

11. Emerging Technologies for Food Safety:
Utilizing innovative technologies such as IoT sensors, data analytics, AI-driven quality control systems, blockchain for supply chain transparency, and rapid pathogen detection methods enhances real-time monitoring, risk assessment, and response capabilities in food safety management.

Conclusion:
Effective food safety and security measures are fundamental to protecting public health, ensuring regulatory compliance, mitigating risks, and maintaining consumer trust in food products. By adhering to food safety regulations, implementing best practices, leveraging technologies, conducting regular audits, and investing in staff training, food businesses contribute to a safer and more resilient food supply chain, benefiting both consumers and the industry as a whole. Continuous vigilance, adaptation to evolving risks, and collaboration across the food ecosystem are key pillars for sustaining high standards of food safety and security in a dynamic global market.

Chapter: Preventing Contamination and Ensuring Food Security

Preventing contamination and ensuring food security are essential components of maintaining public health, consumer trust, and the integrity of the food supply chain. This chapter explores proactive measures, best practices, and technologies aimed at preventing contamination and enhancing food security across various stages of food production, processing, distribution, and consumption.

1. Comprehensive Risk Assessment:
Conducting thorough risk assessments is the foundation of effective contamination prevention and food security strategies. Identify potential hazards (biological, chemical, physical), evaluate risks at each stage of the food supply chain, and prioritize mitigation efforts based on severity and likelihood of occurrence.

2. Adherence to Good Agricultural Practices (GAPs):

In agricultural settings, implementing Good Agricultural Practices is crucial to prevent contamination from farm to fork. This includes proper soil and water management, hygiene practices during harvesting, storage, and transportation, pest control measures, and use of safe agricultural inputs (fertilizers, pesticides).

3. Hygienic Food Handling Practices:
Food handlers and processors must follow strict hygiene practices to prevent cross-contamination, microbial growth, and chemical hazards. This includes regular handwashing, proper sanitation of equipment and surfaces, wearing protective gear (gloves, hairnets), and maintaining temperature control during food handling and storage.

4. Hazard Analysis and Critical Control Points (HACCP):
Implementing HACCP principles involves identifying critical control points in food production processes where hazards can be prevented, eliminated, or reduced to safe levels. Establish monitoring procedures, corrective actions, verification processes, and record-keeping to ensure HACCP effectiveness.

5. Food Safety Training and Certification:
Provide comprehensive training programs for food handlers, processors, and managers on food safety principles, hygiene practices, allergen management, sanitation protocols, and emergency response procedures. Encourage continuous learning, certification (e.g., ServSafe), and adherence to industry standards.

6. Allergen Management and Labeling:

Accurate allergen labeling on food packaging is crucial to prevent allergic reactions in susceptible individuals. Implement strict allergen control measures in production facilities, segregate allergens, clean equipment thoroughly between batches, and educate staff on allergen handling protocols.

7. Enhanced Food Traceability Systems:
Utilize advanced technologies such as blockchain, RFID tags, barcodes, and traceability software to track food products throughout the supply chain. Enhancing traceability enables rapid identification of contamination sources, facilitates targeted recalls, and promotes transparency for consumers.

8. Supplier Verification and Quality Assurance:
Establish rigorous supplier verification processes to ensure that raw materials, ingredients, and food products sourced from suppliers meet quality, safety, and regulatory standards. Conduct audits, inspections, and testing to verify compliance with specifications and mitigate contamination risks.

9. Integrated Pest Management (IPM):
Implement IPM strategies combining biological, mechanical, and chemical control methods to manage pests effectively while minimizing environmental impact and food safety risks. Regular monitoring, pest exclusion measures, sanitation practices, and employee training are key components of IPM.

10. Crisis Preparedness and Response Plans:
Develop comprehensive crisis preparedness and response plans for food contamination incidents, outbreaks, recalls, or emergencies. Define roles, communication channels, escalation procedures, media relations protocols, and collaborate with regulatory agencies for coordinated response efforts.

11. Public Awareness and Consumer Education:
Engage in public awareness campaigns, consumer education initiatives, and transparent communication about food safety practices, labeling information, product recalls, and handling guidelines. Empower consumers to make informed choices, recognize food safety risks, and report concerns.

Conclusion:
Preventing contamination and ensuring food security require a multi-faceted approach encompassing risk assessment, good practices, training, technology adoption, supply chain management, crisis readiness, and consumer engagement. By fostering a culture of food safety, collaboration among stakeholders, regulatory compliance, and continuous improvement, the food industry can uphold high standards of quality, integrity, and safety in food production and distribution, contributing to public health and trust in food systems. Regular monitoring, audits, and adaptation to emerging risks further strengthen resilience and responsiveness in addressing food safety challenges in a dynamic global environment.

Chapter: Social Security and Welfare

Understanding Social Security Systems Worldwide

Social security and welfare programs play a crucial role in providing economic support, healthcare, and social services to individuals and families, particularly during times of need or vulnerability. This chapter explores the principles, components, challenges, and global variations of social security systems, highlighting their importance in promoting social equity, economic stability, and well-being.

1. Principles of Social Security:
Social security is based on fundamental principles aimed at ensuring social protection, reducing poverty, promoting social inclusion, and enhancing quality of life. Key principles include universality (coverage for all), equity, adequacy of benefits, solidarity (shared responsibility), and sustainability (long-term viability).

2. Components of Social Security Systems:
Social security systems typically comprise various components addressing different aspects of social protection:

Income Security: Providing retirement benefits, disability benefits, unemployment benefits, and survivor benefits to individuals and families facing income loss due to retirement, disability, job loss, or death of a breadwinner.

Healthcare Coverage: Ensuring access to affordable healthcare services, medical treatment, preventive care, and pharmaceuticals through public health insurance, national healthcare systems, or subsidized healthcare programs.

Family and Child Support: Offering childcare subsidies, maternity/paternity leave benefits, family allowances, and social services to support families in raising children, promoting work-life balance, and addressing family-related needs.

Social Assistance: Providing means-tested benefits, housing assistance, food assistance (e.g., food stamps), social welfare programs, and emergency relief to individuals and families facing financial hardship or social exclusion.

Employment Services: Offering job training, vocational rehabilitation, job placement assistance, and unemployment counseling to help individuals re-enter the workforce, acquire skills, and achieve economic self-sufficiency.

3. Global Variations in Social Security Systems:

Social security systems vary significantly across countries based on historical, cultural, political, and economic factors. Variations include the extent of coverage, types of benefits offered, funding mechanisms (tax-based, social insurance, public-private partnerships), eligibility criteria, administration models, and level of social protection.

Universal Healthcare Systems: Countries such as Canada, the UK, Australia, and many European nations have universal healthcare systems providing comprehensive healthcare coverage to all residents, funded through taxation or social insurance contributions.

Social Insurance Systems: Countries like Germany, France, Japan, and Sweden have social insurance systems combining contributions from employers, employees, and government to fund benefits such as pensions, healthcare, unemployment, and disability.

Mixed Systems: Some countries adopt mixed models incorporating elements of social insurance and social assistance, tailored to address specific demographic, economic, or social challenges. Examples include the U.S. with Social Security, Medicare, Medicaid, and welfare programs.

Emerging Economies: Developing countries often face challenges in expanding social security coverage due to resource constraints, informal economies, administrative capacity issues, and demographic pressures. Efforts focus on targeted social assistance, healthcare initiatives, and capacity-building for sustainable social protection.

4. Challenges and Future Trends:

Despite the vital role of social security systems, challenges persist, including aging populations, rising healthcare costs, income inequality, informality in labor markets, fiscal sustainability concerns, technological disruptions, and global crises (e.g., pandemics, economic downturns). Future trends in social security include digitalization of services, data analytics for program efficiency, innovative financing models, sustainable pension reforms, social protection floors for vulnerable groups, and global cooperation on social security standards and best practices.

Conclusion:

Social security and welfare systems serve as pillars of social protection, economic stability, and human dignity, promoting inclusive societies and resilient communities. Understanding the principles, components, and global variations of social security systems is essential for policymakers, stakeholders, and citizens to advocate for equitable, sustainable, and effective social protection measures that uphold fundamental rights, mitigate risks, and foster prosperity for present and future generations. Collaborative efforts, evidence-based policies, social dialogue, and international cooperation are vital in addressing emerging challenges and advancing the goals of social security worldwide.

Chapter: Safeguarding Social Welfare Programs Against Fraud

Ensuring the integrity and effectiveness of social welfare programs is crucial for promoting social equity, supporting vulnerable populations, and maintaining public trust in social safety nets. However, these programs are susceptible to various types of fraud and abuse. This chapter explores strategies, technologies, and best practices for safeguarding social welfare programs against fraud, waste, and abuse.

1. Understanding Fraud in Social Welfare Programs:

Fraud in social welfare programs involves intentional deception or misrepresentation by individuals or entities to unlawfully obtain benefits, funds, or services. Common types of fraud include identity theft, falsifying eligibility information, misusing benefits, collusion, and exploitation of loopholes in program rules.

2. Impact of Fraud on Social Welfare Programs:
Fraudulent activities not only drain financial resources meant for genuine beneficiaries but also undermine the effectiveness, sustainability, and public confidence in social welfare programs. Fraud-related losses lead to budgetary strains, reduced program accessibility, increased scrutiny, and potential legal consequences for perpetrators.

3. Strategies for Fraud Prevention and Detection:
a. Risk Assessment: Conduct comprehensive risk assessments to identify vulnerabilities, fraud indicators, high-risk areas, and potential fraud schemes specific to each welfare program.
b. Fraud Analytics: Implement advanced data analytics, AI-driven algorithms, predictive modeling, and anomaly detection techniques to analyze large volumes of data for identifying patterns, anomalies, and suspicious activities indicative of fraud.
c. Identity Verification: Strengthen identity verification processes using biometric authentication, document validation, identity matching tools, and verification against government databases to ensure that applicants and beneficiaries are legitimate.
d. Fraud Detection Tools: Deploy fraud detection software, case management systems, fraud scoring models, and real-time monitoring solutions to flag suspicious transactions, activities, or deviations from typical behavior.

e. Cross-Agency Collaboration: Foster collaboration among government agencies, law enforcement, financial institutions, and anti-fraud organizations to share intelligence, collaborate on investigations, and coordinate efforts in combating fraud across multiple programs.

f. Fraud Awareness and Training: Educate program staff, beneficiaries, and stakeholders about fraud risks, detection methods, reporting mechanisms, whistleblower protections, and the consequences of fraudulent activities.

g. Audit and Compliance Checks: Conduct regular audits, compliance reviews, program evaluations, and performance assessments to ensure adherence to program rules, eligibility criteria, documentation requirements, and internal controls.

h. Fraud Hotlines and Reporting Channels: Establish confidential fraud hotlines, online reporting portals, and whistleblower protection mechanisms to encourage reporting of suspected fraud, waste, or abuse by employees, beneficiaries, or the public.

4. Legal and Enforcement Measures:
Collaborate with legal authorities, prosecutors, and regulatory agencies to investigate fraud allegations, prosecute offenders, recover misappropriated funds, impose penalties, and deter future fraudulent activities through enforcement actions and legal remedies.

5. Technology Solutions for Fraud Prevention:
a. Blockchain Technology: Explore blockchain-based solutions for secure, transparent, and immutable record-keeping, enhancing transparency, auditability, and trust in benefit distribution processes.

b. Machine Learning and AI: Leverage machine learning algorithms, artificial intelligence, pattern recognition, and anomaly detection models to automate fraud detection, reduce false positives, and improve decision-making in fraud investigations.

c. Biometric Authentication: Implement biometric authentication systems (fingerprint, facial recognition) for identity verification, reducing the risk of identity theft, unauthorized access, and impersonation in welfare programs.
d. Data Integration and Sharing: Integrate data from multiple sources (government databases, financial institutions, employment records) to perform comprehensive beneficiary eligibility checks, income verification, and fraud risk assessments.

6. Public-Private Partnerships and Innovation:
Engage with private sector partners, technology vendors, fintech companies, and academia to leverage innovative solutions, data analytics tools, cybersecurity expertise, and best practices in fraud prevention and detection tailored to social welfare programs' unique challenges.

Conclusion:
Safeguarding social welfare programs against fraud requires a multifaceted approach encompassing risk assessment, fraud detection technologies, collaboration, education, legal measures, and technological innovation. By adopting proactive fraud prevention strategies, leveraging data analytics insights, strengthening identity verification processes, promoting transparency, and fostering a culture of integrity and compliance, governments and organizations can protect scarce resources, improve program efficiency, and ensure that social welfare benefits reach those truly in need, preserving public trust and social welfare objectives in the long term.

Chapter: Freedom and Security

Balancing Freedom and Security in the Digital Age

In the modern digital landscape, the pursuit of freedom and security has become increasingly intertwined and complex. This chapter delves into the challenges, tensions, and strategies for achieving a delicate balance between safeguarding individual freedoms and ensuring robust security measures in the context of evolving technological advancements and global interconnectedness.

1. Fundamental Rights and Freedoms:
a. Privacy Rights: Individuals have the right to control their personal data, limit surveillance, and maintain confidentiality in their communications, transactions, and online activities.

b. Freedom of Expression: Upholding freedom of speech, opinion, creativity, and access to information without undue censorship, surveillance, or restrictions is essential in democratic societies.

c. Civil Liberties: Protecting civil liberties such as due process, freedom from discrimination, and access to justice strengthens the rule of law, accountability, and democratic governance.

2. Security Imperatives in the Digital Era:

a. Cyber Threats: Rapid technological advancements, interconnected systems, and digital dependencies expose individuals, organizations, and nations to cyber threats such as hacking, data breaches, cyber espionage, and ransomware attacks.

b. National Security: Governments and law enforcement agencies have a responsibility to protect national security, critical infrastructure, public safety, and economic interests from cyber threats, terrorism, and foreign interference.

c. Regulatory Frameworks: Implementing cybersecurity regulations, data protection laws (e.g., GDPR, CCPA), surveillance measures, and law enforcement capabilities is crucial for combating cybercrime, ensuring data privacy, and maintaining societal resilience.

3. Challenges in Balancing Freedom and Security:

a. Surveillance Dilemma: Balancing the need for surveillance (for security purposes) with preserving privacy rights and preventing mass surveillance abuses poses ethical, legal, and societal challenges.

b. Encryption Debate: The tension between advocating for strong encryption (protecting privacy and security) and addressing law enforcement's legitimate needs for access to encrypted data for criminal investigations highlights the encryption policy debate.

c. Cybersecurity vs. Civil Liberties: Implementing robust cybersecurity measures (e.g., monitoring, threat intelligence, access controls) may conflict with individual freedoms, transparency, and accountability if not balanced appropriately.

4. Strategies for Balance and Harmonization:
a. Legislative Clarity: Develop clear, transparent, and proportionate legal frameworks, regulations, and oversight mechanisms that strike a balance between security imperatives and individual rights.
b. Privacy by Design: Embed privacy and security principles into technological designs, data handling practices, and policy frameworks to ensure data protection, user consent, and minimization of data collection.
c. Encryption Standards: Promote international dialogue, industry collaboration, and consensus-building on encryption standards, lawful access mechanisms, and responsible encryption practices that uphold security and privacy principles.
d. Ethical AI and Surveillance: Implement ethical guidelines, human rights impact assessments, and oversight mechanisms for AI technologies, surveillance tools, biometrics, and facial recognition systems to mitigate risks of abuse, discrimination, and privacy violations.
e. Transparency and Accountability: Foster transparency in government surveillance practices, data collection practices, use of surveillance technologies, and accountability mechanisms through independent oversight, judicial review, and public reporting.
f. Multistakeholder Collaboration: Engage in inclusive dialogue, partnerships, and consultations among governments, industry stakeholders, civil society, academia, and international organizations to address complex challenges, share best practices, and uphold human rights in digital environments.

5. Education and Awareness:
Promote digital literacy, cybersecurity awareness, privacy education, and informed civic engagement among individuals, communities, businesses, and policymakers to empower informed decision-making, responsible digital citizenship, and advocacy for rights-based approaches.

Conclusion:
Balancing freedom and security in the digital age requires nuanced approaches, collaboration, and ongoing adaptation to evolving threats and technological landscapes. By embracing principles of transparency, accountability, proportionality, human rights, and ethical governance, societies can navigate the complexities of digital freedoms and security imperatives while fostering innovation, trust, and resilience in interconnected digital ecosystems. Striking this delicate balance is essential for upholding democratic values, protecting individual liberties, and ensuring collective security in an increasingly interconnected and digital world.

Chapter: Privacy vs. Surveillance: Debates and Considerations

The ongoing debate between privacy and surveillance is at the forefront of discussions in the digital age, shaping policies, technology development, and societal norms. This chapter explores the nuances, ethical considerations, challenges, and implications surrounding the balance between individual privacy rights and the need for surveillance in various contexts.

1. Defining Privacy and Surveillance:

a. Privacy: Privacy encompasses individuals' rights to control their personal information, autonomy, anonymity, and decision-making regarding data collection, use, and disclosure.

b. Surveillance: Surveillance refers to systematic monitoring, tracking, data collection, and analysis of individuals, groups, or activities, often conducted by governments, corporations, or other entities for security, intelligence, or commercial purposes.

2. Ethical Considerations:

a. Informed Consent: Surveillance practices should respect individuals' rights to informed consent, transparency, and awareness regarding data collection, surveillance methods, and potential impacts on privacy.

b. Proportionality: Surveillance measures should be proportionate to the legitimate aims they seek to achieve, avoiding overreach, mass surveillance, or indiscriminate data collection.

c. Purpose Limitation: Data collected through surveillance should be used only for specified, lawful purposes, preventing misuse, profiling, or discriminatory practices.

d. Accountability and Oversight: Establishing robust accountability mechanisms, legal safeguards, independent oversight, and judicial review processes is crucial to prevent abuses, protect rights, and ensure accountability for surveillance activities.

3. Surveillance for National Security:

a. Terrorism and Threat Detection: Governments employ surveillance measures (e.g., intelligence gathering, monitoring communications) to detect and prevent terrorist activities, national security threats, cyberattacks, and organized crime.

b. Balancing Rights: Balancing national security imperatives with individual rights requires clear legal frameworks, oversight mechanisms, transparency, and checks on surveillance powers to prevent abuses and protect civil liberties.

4. Corporate Surveillance and Data Privacy:
a. Data Collection Practices: Corporations engage in extensive data collection, profiling, behavioral tracking, and data analytics for marketing, targeted advertising, user profiling, and product customization.
b. User Consent and Transparency: Ensuring user consent, transparent data practices, data minimization, encryption, and adherence to data protection regulations (e.g., GDPR, CCPA) are essential for safeguarding consumer privacy rights in the digital marketplace.

5. Technological Advances and Privacy Challenges:
a. Biometrics and Facial Recognition: Advancements in biometric technologies raise concerns about surveillance, facial recognition accuracy, privacy infringements, bias, and potential misuse in public and private settings.
b. Internet of Things (IoT): Proliferation of IoT devices collecting vast amounts of personal data poses privacy risks related to data security, user consent, data sharing, and potential exploitation of IoT ecosystems for surveillance purposes.

6. Protecting Privacy Rights:
a. Encryption and Anonymity: Promoting strong encryption standards, anonymization techniques, secure communication protocols, and privacy-enhancing technologies (PETs) safeguards individual privacy, data confidentiality, and freedom of expression.

b. Legislative and Regulatory Measures: Governments and international bodies enact data protection laws, privacy regulations, cybersecurity standards, and privacy-enhancing policies to protect privacy rights, limit surveillance abuses, and ensure accountability in data handling practices.

7. Public Perception and Awareness:
a. Digital Literacy: Enhancing public awareness, digital literacy, privacy education, and empowerment initiatives enable individuals to make informed choices, protect their privacy online, and advocate for privacy-enhancing policies.
b. Civil Society and Advocacy: Engaging civil society, privacy advocates, academia, and technology experts in policy debates, transparency initiatives, public consultations, and privacy impact assessments strengthens privacy protections, accountability, and democratic governance in surveillance practices.

Conclusion:
Navigating the complex interplay between privacy and surveillance requires thoughtful deliberation, ethical frameworks, legal safeguards, technological innovation, and informed public discourse. Striking a balance that upholds individual privacy rights, promotes transparency, accountability, and proportionality in surveillance practices, and addresses legitimate security concerns is essential for fostering trust, preserving civil liberties, and advancing responsible use of surveillance technologies in democratic societies. Continuous dialogue, interdisciplinary collaboration, regulatory vigilance, and societal awareness empower stakeholders to navigate these challenges while upholding fundamental rights and values in the digital era.

Chapter: The Future of Security

Emerging Trends and Technologies in Security

The landscape of security is continually evolving, driven by technological advancements, global challenges, and evolving threat landscapes. This chapter explores key emerging trends, innovative technologies, and evolving paradigms shaping the future of security across various domains, from cybersecurity to physical security and beyond.

1. Cybersecurity in a Connected World:
a. Zero Trust Architecture: Adopting Zero Trust principles, where no entity is inherently trusted, and strict access controls, identity verification, continuous monitoring, and least privilege principles are implemented to mitigate insider threats and unauthorized access.

b. AI-Powered Security: Leveraging artificial intelligence (AI) and machine learning (ML) algorithms for advanced threat detection, behavioral analytics, anomaly detection, and automated response capabilities to combat sophisticated cyber threats and reduce response times.

c. Cloud Security: Enhancing cloud security posture through robust encryption, secure access management, workload protection, cloud-native security tools, and continuous monitoring for compliance and threat detection in cloud environments.

2. Internet of Things (IoT) Security Challenges:

a. IoT Device Security: Implementing secure-by-design principles, device authentication, firmware updates, network segmentation, and IoT security frameworks to mitigate vulnerabilities, unauthorized access, and IoT-based attacks targeting smart homes, industrial IoT, and critical infrastructure.

b. Edge Computing Security: Addressing security risks in edge computing environments by deploying edge security solutions, encryption protocols, secure data processing, and real-time threat detection at the network edge to protect data and devices.

3. Data Privacy and Compliance:

a. Privacy-Enhancing Technologies (PETs): Deploying PETs such as differential privacy, homomorphic encryption, decentralized identity management, and data anonymization techniques to protect user privacy, comply with data protection regulations (e.g., GDPR, CCPA), and foster trust in data handling practices.

b. Blockchain for Data Integrity: Utilizing blockchain technology for secure, tamper-proof data storage, transparent audit trails, smart contracts, and identity verification to enhance data integrity, reduce fraud, and enable secure data sharing across networks.

4. Physical Security Innovations:
a. Biometric Access Control: Advancements in biometric authentication (fingerprint, facial recognition, iris scanning) for access control systems, surveillance monitoring, and identity verification to enhance physical security measures in critical infrastructure, airports, and high-security facilities.
b. AI-Powered Video Analytics: Leveraging AI-driven video analytics, object recognition, behavior analysis, and real-time threat detection in video surveillance systems to improve situational awareness, response times, and security incident management.

5. Emerging Threats and Response Strategies:
a. Ransomware Defense: Enhancing ransomware defenses through secure backups, ransomware detection tools, network segmentation, employee training, incident response plans, and collaboration with cybersecurity firms and law enforcement agencies for threat intelligence sharing and response coordination.
b. Supply Chain Security: Strengthening supply chain security through vendor risk assessments, supply chain visibility tools, secure communication channels, supply chain resilience planning, and adherence to cybersecurity standards and best practices across the supply chain ecosystem.
c. Deepfakes and Misinformation: Developing deepfake detection tools, media authentication techniques, digital forensics capabilities, and media literacy programs to combat the spread of fake news, misinformation, and manipulated media content in social media and digital platforms.

6. Collaboration and Resilience:

a. Public-Private Partnerships: Fostering collaboration among government agencies, industry partners, academia, cybersecurity organizations, and international bodies for threat intelligence sharing, incident response coordination, cybersecurity awareness campaigns, and capacity-building initiatives.

b. Cyber Resilience Frameworks: Implementing cyber resilience frameworks (e.g., NIST Cybersecurity Framework, ISO/IEC 27001) encompassing risk management, incident response planning, business continuity, secure software development practices, employee training, and continuous security monitoring to enhance organizational resilience against cyber threats.

7. Ethical Considerations and Human-Centric Security:

a. Ethical AI and Bias Mitigation: Addressing ethical considerations in AI-powered security systems, bias mitigation, fairness, transparency, accountability, and human oversight to ensure responsible use of AI technologies in security applications without compromising privacy, rights, or equity.

b. User-Centric Security Design: Prioritizing user experience, usability, accessibility, and privacy preferences in security design, authentication mechanisms, data handling practices, and cybersecurity education to empower individuals in protecting their digital identities and assets.

Conclusion:

The future of security is intertwined with technological innovation, strategic foresight, collaborative partnerships, and a human-centric approach to addressing evolving threats and challenges. Embracing emerging trends such as AI-powered security, IoT security best practices, data privacy technologies, and resilient cybersecurity frameworks equips organizations and societies to navigate complex security landscapes, safeguard critical assets, protect user privacy rights, and foster trust in digital ecosystems. Continuous adaptation, vigilance, education, and ethical stewardship are essential in shaping a secure, resilient, and inclusive digital future for all stakeholders in an interconnected world.

Chapter: Empowering Readers to Stay Safe and Secure in an Evolving World

In today's rapidly evolving digital landscape, staying safe and secure requires proactive awareness, informed decision-making, and practical strategies to mitigate risks across various domains. This chapter empowers readers with essential knowledge, practical tips, and recommended practices to enhance their personal and digital security in an interconnected world.

1. Digital Hygiene Practices:
a. Strong Password Management: Use complex, unique passwords for each account, consider using a reputable password manager, and enable two-factor authentication (2FA) where available to add an extra layer of security.
b. Regular Software Updates: Keep operating systems, applications, antivirus software, and firmware updated to patch vulnerabilities and protect against exploits and malware.
c. Phishing Awareness: Be cautious of suspicious emails, messages, and links; verify sender identities; avoid sharing sensitive information or clicking on unfamiliar attachments or links.
d. Secure Network Connections: Use encrypted Wi-Fi networks (WPA2/WPA3), avoid public Wi-Fi for sensitive activities, and consider using a virtual private network (VPN) for added privacy and security.

2. Privacy Protection Strategies:
a. Privacy Settings Review: Regularly review and adjust privacy settings on social media platforms, apps, and devices to control data sharing, visibility, and permissions.
b. Data Minimization: Minimize personal information shared online, limit exposure of sensitive details, and be cautious of oversharing on social media or public forums.

c. Privacy-Focused Tools: Use privacy-enhancing browser extensions, ad blockers, tracker blockers, and encrypted communication apps to protect online privacy and reduce tracking.
d. Data Backup: Regularly back up important data (documents, photos, files) to secure cloud storage or external devices to prevent data loss from hardware failures, ransomware attacks, or accidents.

3. Cybersecurity Best Practices:
a. Awareness Training: Stay informed about common cyber threats, phishing techniques, social engineering tactics, and cybersecurity trends through reputable sources, training programs, and security awareness campaigns.
b. Safe Online Shopping: Shop from trusted websites with secure payment gateways (look for HTTPS), avoid sharing payment information over unsecured connections, and monitor financial statements for unauthorized transactions.
c. Device Security: Secure devices (computers, smartphones, IoT devices) with antivirus software, firewalls, device encryption, and remote wipe capabilities in case of theft or loss.
d. Data Encryption: Encrypt sensitive data at rest and in transit using encryption tools, secure messaging apps, and encrypted email services to protect data confidentiality from unauthorized access.

4. Social Engineering Awareness:
a. Phishing Defense: Be skeptical of unexpected emails, messages, or calls requesting personal information, passwords, or financial details; verify requests through official channels before sharing sensitive information.
b. Impersonation Detection: Verify identities of individuals or organizations requesting access, credentials, or sensitive information; confirm legitimacy through known contact methods or by contacting the organization directly.

c. Social Media Caution: Be cautious of social engineering tactics on social media (fake profiles, scams, phishing links); avoid sharing personal details, travel plans, or financial information publicly.

5. Physical Security Measures:
a. Securing Physical Spaces: Implement physical security measures such as locks, alarms, security cameras, and access control systems to protect homes, offices, and personal belongings.
b. Data Disposal: Safely dispose of sensitive documents, electronic devices, and storage media by shredding paper documents, wiping data from devices before disposal, and using secure data erasure methods.
c. Safe Social Practices: Be mindful of sharing location information, personal activities, or travel plans on social media; consider privacy implications and potential security risks of publicizing personal details.

6. Continuous Learning and Adaptation:
a. Stay Informed: Keep abreast of evolving cybersecurity threats, privacy regulations, and security best practices through reliable news sources, cybersecurity blogs, industry reports, and online forums.
b. Seek Professional Advice: Consult cybersecurity experts, IT professionals, or privacy specialists for personalized security assessments, risk mitigation strategies, and guidance on securing digital assets and online activities.
c. Report Suspicious Activities: Report cybersecurity incidents, fraud attempts, identity theft, or suspicious online behavior to relevant authorities, cybersecurity agencies, or consumer protection agencies for assistance and investigation.

Conclusion:

Empowering readers to stay safe and secure in an evolving world requires a proactive approach, continuous education, and adoption of practical security measures across digital, physical, and social domains. By implementing strong digital hygiene practices, protecting privacy online, staying vigilant against cyber threats, fostering awareness of social engineering tactics, securing physical spaces, and embracing a mindset of lifelong learning and adaptation, individuals can navigate the digital landscape with confidence, resilience, and enhanced security posture. Remember, security is a shared responsibility, and proactive measures contribute to a safer and more secure digital ecosystem for everyone.

BONUS CHAPTERS

Chapter: Encryption

Encryption plays a pivotal role in safeguarding sensitive information, securing communications, and protecting digital privacy in an interconnected world. This chapter delves into the fundamentals of encryption, its applications across various domains, evolving encryption standards, and the importance of encryption in maintaining data confidentiality and security.

1. Understanding Encryption Basics:
Encryption is the process of converting plaintext data into ciphertext using cryptographic algorithms and keys, rendering it unreadable to unauthorized users. The decryption process reverses encryption, converting ciphertext back to plaintext using the appropriate decryption keys.

2. Components of Encryption:
a. Cipher: The mathematical algorithm used for encryption and decryption, such as AES (Advanced Encryption Standard), RSA (Rivest-Shamir-Adleman), or ECC (Elliptic Curve Cryptography).
b. Key: The secret value used by the encryption algorithm to transform plaintext into ciphertext and vice versa. Keys can be symmetric (shared key for encryption and decryption) or asymmetric (public-private key pairs for encryption and decryption).

3. Applications of Encryption:
a. Data Security: Encrypting sensitive data at rest (stored data) and in transit (data being transmitted) protects against unauthorized access, data breaches, and eavesdropping.

b. Secure Communication: Encrypting emails, instant messages, voice calls, and file transfers using encryption protocols (e.g., SSL/TLS, PGP, Signal Protocol) ensures privacy and confidentiality in communication channels.

c. Disk Encryption: Encrypting hard drives, storage devices, and removable media (e.g., USB drives) prevents data theft, unauthorized access, and data leakage in case of device loss or theft.

d. Cloud Security: Employing encryption for data stored in cloud services (e.g., AES-256 encryption for cloud storage) ensures data privacy, compliance with regulations, and protection against cloud breaches.

4. Types of Encryption:

a. Symmetric Encryption: Uses a single shared key for both encryption and decryption operations, offering fast processing speeds for bulk data encryption (e.g., AES, DES, 3DES).

b. Asymmetric Encryption: Utilizes public-private key pairs, where the public key encrypts data, and the private key decrypts it. Commonly used in digital signatures, secure communication (e.g., RSA, ECC).

c. Hashing: Hash functions convert data into fixed-length hash values, used for data integrity verification, password hashing (e.g., SHA-256, bcrypt), and digital signatures (e.g., HMAC).

d. End-to-End Encryption (E2EE): Ensures that data is encrypted on the sender's device, transmitted encrypted, and decrypted only on the recipient's device, preventing intermediaries from accessing plaintext data (e.g., Signal, WhatsApp E2EE chats).

5. Encryption Standards and Protocols:

a. AES (Advanced Encryption Standard): Widely adopted symmetric encryption algorithm known for its security, efficiency, and flexibility in key lengths (128-bit, 256-bit).

b. TLS (Transport Layer Security): Protocols like TLS 1.2 and TLS 1.3 secure communication over networks (e.g., HTTPS) using encryption, authentication, and key exchange mechanisms.

c. PGP (Pretty Good Privacy): A popular encryption program for email encryption, digital signatures, and secure file transfer, based on asymmetric encryption principles.

d. VPN Encryption: Virtual Private Networks (VPNs) use encryption protocols (e.g., OpenVPN, IPSec) to create secure, encrypted tunnels for private and anonymous internet browsing and remote access.

6. Challenges and Considerations:

a. Key Management: Secure storage, distribution, and management of encryption keys are crucial to prevent key compromise, unauthorized decryption, and data exposure.

b. Performance Impact: Strong encryption algorithms may impose computational overhead, latency, and resource utilization, requiring optimization strategies for performance-critical systems.

c. Backdoor Risks: Intentional or unintentional backdoors in encryption systems pose risks to security and privacy, emphasizing the importance of open, audited encryption standards.

d. Quantum Computing: Advancements in quantum computing pose challenges to traditional encryption methods (e.g., RSA, ECC), driving research into quantum-resistant encryption algorithms (e.g., post-quantum cryptography).

7. Importance of Encryption:

a. Data Privacy: Protects sensitive personal, financial, and business data from unauthorized access, breaches, identity theft, and surveillance.

b. Compliance: Supports regulatory compliance requirements (e.g., GDPR, HIPAA, PCI DSS) for data protection, privacy, and secure transmission.

c. Trust and Confidentiality: Fosters trust among users, customers, and stakeholders by ensuring confidentiality, integrity, and authenticity of data and communications.
d. National Security: Plays a crucial role in securing critical infrastructure, government communications, defense systems, and classified information against cyber threats and espionage.

Conclusion:
Encryption is a cornerstone of modern cybersecurity, ensuring data confidentiality, integrity, and privacy in an interconnected digital world. Understanding encryption principles, implementing strong encryption standards, secure key management practices, and adopting encryption technologies across networks, devices, and applications are essential steps in safeguarding sensitive information, maintaining trust, and strengthening security posture against evolving cyber threats and data breaches. Encryption empowers individuals, organizations, and nations to protect their digital assets, privacy rights, and critical infrastructure in an increasingly digital and interconnected environment.

Chapter: Cryptographic Algorithms

Cryptographic algorithms form the backbone of modern encryption and security protocols, providing essential tools for protecting sensitive data, ensuring secure communication, and maintaining digital privacy. This chapter explores different types of cryptographic algorithms, their functionalities, strengths, vulnerabilities, and real-world applications across various security domains.

1. Symmetric Encryption Algorithms:
Symmetric encryption algorithms use a single shared key for both encryption and decryption operations. They are efficient for bulk data encryption and are widely used in securing data at rest and in transit.

Advanced Encryption Standard (AES): A symmetric block cipher adopted as the standard encryption algorithm by governments and industries worldwide. AES supports key lengths of 128-bit, 192-bit, and 256-bit, offering strong security and performance.

Data Encryption Standard (DES) and Triple DES (3DES): Legacy symmetric encryption standards, DES uses a 56-bit key, while 3DES applies DES encryption three times with different keys, enhancing security but with increased computational overhead.

2. Asymmetric Encryption Algorithms:
Asymmetric encryption algorithms use public-private key pairs for encryption and decryption operations, providing a secure way to exchange keys and establish secure communication channels.

Rivest-Shamir-Adleman (RSA): A widely used asymmetric encryption algorithm for digital signatures, key exchange, and secure communication. RSA relies on the difficulty of factoring large prime numbers for its security.

Elliptic Curve Cryptography (ECC): An asymmetric encryption scheme based on elliptic curves over finite fields, ECC offers strong security with shorter key lengths compared to RSA, making it suitable for resource-constrained environments.

3. Hash Functions:
Hash functions are one-way cryptographic algorithms that map input data of arbitrary size to fixed-size hash values, used for data integrity verification, password hashing, digital signatures, and message authentication codes (MACs).

Secure Hash Algorithm (SHA): SHA-256, SHA-384, and SHA-512 are widely used hash functions for data integrity checks, digital signatures, and blockchain technology.

Message Digest Algorithm (MD5): A legacy hash function vulnerable to collision attacks, MD5 is no longer recommended for security-sensitive applications due to its weaknesses.

4. Key Exchange and Authentication Algorithms:
Key exchange algorithms facilitate secure key exchange between parties to establish secure communication channels, while authentication algorithms verify the identity of communicating parties.

Diffie-Hellman Key Exchange (DH): A key agreement protocol allowing two parties to establish a shared secret key over an insecure channel, used in secure communication protocols like TLS/SSL.

Digital Signature Algorithm (DSA): An asymmetric algorithm used for digital signatures and authentication, ensuring message integrity, non-repudiation, and verification of sender identity.

5. Cryptographic Protocols and Standards:
Cryptographic protocols combine cryptographic algorithms with specific rules and procedures to achieve secure communication, data protection, and cryptographic operations.

Transport Layer Security (TLS) and Secure Sockets Layer (SSL): Protocols providing secure communication over networks using symmetric and asymmetric encryption, key exchange, and digital certificates for authentication and data privacy (e.g., HTTPS for secure web browsing).

Pretty Good Privacy (PGP): A protocol for email encryption, digital signatures, and secure communication, based on asymmetric encryption principles and key management.

6. Cryptographic Vulnerabilities and Best Practices:
Understanding cryptographic vulnerabilities such as brute-force attacks, key management flaws, algorithm weaknesses, and implementation errors is crucial for designing secure cryptographic systems.

Key Management: Secure storage, generation, distribution, and rotation of cryptographic keys are essential for maintaining confidentiality, integrity, and availability of encrypted data.

Algorithm Selection: Choosing strong cryptographic algorithms with sufficient key lengths, robustness against attacks, and adherence to industry standards and best practices is paramount for ensuring security resilience.

Conclusion:

Cryptographic algorithms form the cornerstone of modern cybersecurity, providing essential mechanisms for data encryption, integrity verification, authentication, and secure communication. By understanding the strengths, vulnerabilities, and real-world applications of cryptographic algorithms, security professionals can design robust encryption schemes, secure communication protocols, and cryptographic systems that protect sensitive information, thwart cyber threats, and uphold privacy rights in an increasingly interconnected digital world. Continuous research, adherence to cryptographic standards, secure implementation practices, and regular security assessments are key to maintaining cryptographic security posture and mitigating evolving cryptographic risks and attacks.

Chapter: Data Protection

Data protection encompasses a range of strategies, technologies, and practices designed to safeguard sensitive information, preserve data integrity, ensure privacy compliance, and mitigate data risks throughout its lifecycle. This chapter explores key aspects of data protection, including data security measures, privacy considerations, regulatory compliance, and best practices for organizations and individuals to protect valuable data assets.

1. Understanding Data Protection:
Data protection refers to the set of measures and protocols implemented to secure data against unauthorized access, data breaches, data loss, and ensure data privacy and confidentiality. It encompasses technical, organizational, and legal frameworks aimed at safeguarding data integrity, availability, and confidentiality.

2. Data Security Measures:
a. Encryption: Utilizing strong encryption algorithms (e.g., AES, RSA) for data at rest and in transit to prevent unauthorized access and data theft.
b. Access Controls: Implementing role-based access controls (RBAC), least privilege principles, and multi-factor authentication (MFA) to limit access to sensitive data based on user roles and permissions.
c. Data Masking and Anonymization: Masking or anonymizing sensitive data in non-production environments to protect privacy during development, testing, and analytics processes.

d. Secure Storage: Using secure storage solutions, encryption keys management, and access logs to protect data stored in databases, cloud environments, and storage devices.

3. Privacy Considerations:
a. Data Minimization: Collecting and processing only necessary data for specified purposes to reduce privacy risks and data exposure.
b. Privacy by Design: Incorporating privacy principles into system architecture, software development, and product design to embed privacy protections by default.
c. Consent Management: Obtaining informed consent for data collection, processing, and sharing activities, and providing options for users to control their data preferences.
d. Data Retention Policies: Establishing policies for data retention periods, archival practices, and secure data disposal to comply with privacy regulations and reduce data retention risks.

4. Regulatory Compliance:
a. General Data Protection Regulation (GDPR): Compliance with GDPR requirements for data protection, privacy rights, data subject consent, data transfers, and breach notifications for organizations handling EU residents' data.
b. California Consumer Privacy Act (CCPA): Adherence to CCPA provisions regarding consumer data rights, transparency, data access requests, opt-out options, and data sale disclosures for businesses operating in California.
c. Health Insurance Portability and Accountability Act (HIPAA): Compliance with HIPAA regulations for protecting health information (PHI), data security standards, privacy practices, and breach notification requirements for healthcare organizations and service providers.

d. Payment Card Industry Data Security Standard (PCI DSS): Compliance with PCI DSS requirements for secure handling, processing, and storage of payment card data to prevent payment fraud and data breaches in financial transactions.

5. Data Protection Best Practices:
a. Data Backup and Recovery: Regular data backups, disaster recovery plans, and testing procedures to ensure data availability, business continuity, and resilience against data loss incidents.
b. Employee Training: Providing data protection awareness, cybersecurity training, and best practices education for employees to recognize data risks, handle data securely, and comply with privacy policies.
c. Security Incident Response: Establishing incident response teams, protocols, and escalation procedures for identifying, mitigating, and responding to data breaches, security incidents, and privacy breaches promptly.
d. Third-Party Risk Management: Assessing and managing data risks associated with third-party vendors, service providers, and data processors through contractual agreements, audits, and security assessments.

6. Emerging Technologies and Data Protection:
a. AI and Machine Learning: Leveraging AI-driven analytics, anomaly detection, and behavior analysis for proactive threat detection, fraud prevention, and data protection insights.
b. Blockchain Technology: Exploring blockchain applications for secure data storage, decentralized identity management, data provenance, and tamper-resistant record-keeping in data-intensive industries.
c. Privacy-Enhancing Technologies (PETs): Implementing PETs such as differential privacy, homomorphic encryption, secure multi-party computation (MPC), and tokenization to enhance data privacy, minimize data exposure, and comply with privacy regulations.

Conclusion:

Data protection is a multifaceted discipline encompassing technical, legal, and organizational measures to safeguard data integrity, confidentiality, and privacy in today's data-driven environments. By adopting robust data security measures, privacy principles, regulatory compliance frameworks, and proactive risk management strategies, organizations can mitigate data risks, build trust with stakeholders, and uphold data protection standards in alignment with evolving privacy regulations and industry best practices. Continuous monitoring, security assessments, and adaptation to emerging data protection technologies and threats are essential for maintaining data resilience and data privacy in a rapidly evolving digital landscape.

Chapter: Cybersecurity

Cybersecurity is a critical field focused on protecting digital systems, networks, and data from cyber threats, unauthorized access, and malicious activities. This chapter explores the fundamentals of cybersecurity, common cyber threats, cybersecurity best practices, and strategies for individuals and organizations to enhance their cyber resilience in an increasingly digital world.

1. Understanding Cybersecurity:
Cybersecurity encompasses technologies, processes, and practices designed to protect computers, networks, data, and digital assets from cyber threats such as malware, phishing, ransomware, hacking, and insider threats. It involves proactive measures to detect, prevent, respond to, and recover from cybersecurity incidents.

2. Common Cyber Threats:
a. Malware: Malicious software such as viruses, worms, Trojans, and ransomware designed to disrupt, damage, or gain unauthorized access to computer systems and data.
b. Phishing and Social Engineering: Deceptive techniques used to trick users into revealing sensitive information, credentials, or installing malicious software through emails, messages, or fake websites.
c. Hacking and Unauthorized Access: Intrusion attempts, exploitation of vulnerabilities, and unauthorized access to networks, systems, or data by cybercriminals or malicious actors.
d. Insider Threats: Malicious or negligent actions by employees, contractors, or insiders leading to data breaches, sabotage, or unauthorized access to sensitive information.

e. Denial-of-Service (DoS) Attacks: Overloading or disrupting network resources, servers, or websites to make them unavailable to legitimate users, often carried out through botnets or network flooding.

3. Cybersecurity Best Practices:
a. Strong Authentication: Implementing multi-factor authentication (MFA), strong passwords, and biometric authentication to verify user identities and prevent unauthorized access.
b. Patch Management: Regularly applying security patches, updates, and fixes to operating systems, software, and applications to address vulnerabilities and reduce attack surfaces.
c. Network Segmentation: Dividing networks into separate segments with access controls, firewalls, and intrusion detection/prevention systems (IDS/IPS) to contain breaches and limit lateral movement by attackers.
d. Data Encryption: Encrypting sensitive data at rest and in transit using strong encryption algorithms (e.g., AES, RSA) to protect data confidentiality and prevent data breaches.
e. Security Awareness Training: Educating employees, users, and stakeholders about cybersecurity risks, phishing prevention, secure browsing habits, and incident reporting procedures to enhance security awareness and resilience.
f. Incident Response Planning: Developing and testing incident response plans, security incident detection, containment, eradication, and recovery procedures to minimize cybersecurity impacts and downtime during incidents.
g. Backup and Recovery: Regularly backing up critical data, systems, and configurations, and testing data recovery processes to ensure business continuity and resilience against data loss incidents, ransomware attacks, or system failures.

4. Cybersecurity Frameworks and Standards:

a. NIST Cybersecurity Framework: Provides a risk-based approach to cybersecurity with guidelines, controls, and best practices for identifying, protecting, detecting, responding to, and recovering from cybersecurity threats and incidents.
b. ISO/IEC 27001: International standard for information security management systems (ISMS) providing a framework for establishing, implementing, maintaining, and improving organizational cybersecurity practices and controls.
c. PCI DSS: Payment Card Industry Data Security Standard outlines security requirements for organizations handling payment card data to prevent payment fraud, data breaches, and secure payment transactions.

5. Emerging Trends in Cybersecurity:
a. AI and Machine Learning in Security: Leveraging AI-driven analytics, behavioral analysis, threat intelligence, and automation for advanced threat detection, anomaly detection, and security incident response.
b. Zero Trust Security Model: Adopting a zero-trust approach with strict access controls, continuous authentication, least privilege access, and micro-segmentation to mitigate insider threats and lateral movement by attackers.
c. Cloud Security: Implementing cloud security best practices, encryption, access controls, and security monitoring for cloud environments to protect cloud data, applications, and infrastructure from cyber threats.
d. IoT Security: Enhancing security for Internet of Things (IoT) devices, networks, and ecosystems with IoT security standards, device authentication, firmware updates, and secure communication protocols to prevent IoT-based attacks and breaches.

Conclusion:

Cybersecurity is a continuous effort that requires proactive measures, risk management strategies, collaboration, and ongoing awareness to protect against evolving cyber threats and digital risks. By adopting cybersecurity best practices, leveraging security frameworks, implementing advanced security technologies, and fostering a culture of security awareness, individuals and organizations can strengthen their cyber resilience, protect valuable data assets, and mitigate the impact of cybersecurity incidents in today's digital age. Collaboration among stakeholders, threat intelligence sharing, and adherence to cybersecurity standards play crucial roles in building a secure and resilient cyber ecosystem for a safer digital future.

Chapter: Cryptography

Cryptography serves as the foundation for secure communication, data protection, and digital trust in today's interconnected world. This chapter explores the principles of cryptography, cryptographic techniques, encryption algorithms, and their applications in securing data, communications, and digital transactions.

1. Understanding Cryptography:
Cryptography is the science and art of securing information through encryption and decryption techniques to ensure confidentiality, integrity, authentication, and non-repudiation of data. It involves converting plaintext data into ciphertext using encryption algorithms and keys, and then reversing the process through decryption to retrieve the original data.

2. Cryptographic Techniques:
a. Encryption: The process of converting plaintext data into ciphertext using cryptographic algorithms and encryption keys. Symmetric encryption uses a single shared key for encryption and decryption (e.g., AES), while asymmetric encryption employs public-private key pairs for secure communication and digital signatures (e.g., RSA, ECC).
b. Hashing: One-way mathematical functions that generate fixed-length hash values (hash codes) from input data. Hash functions (e.g., SHA-256, MD5) are used for data integrity verification, password hashing, and digital signatures.
c. Digital Signatures: Cryptographic signatures generated using private keys to verify the authenticity, integrity, and non-repudiation of digital messages, documents, and transactions.

d. Key Exchange: Secure methods for exchanging cryptographic keys between parties, ensuring confidentiality, and enabling encrypted communication sessions (e.g., Diffie-Hellman key exchange).

3. Encryption Algorithms:
a. Advanced Encryption Standard (AES): A symmetric block cipher widely adopted for its security, efficiency, and scalability. AES supports key lengths of 128-bit, 192-bit, and 256-bit, providing strong encryption for data at rest and in transit.
b. Rivest-Shamir-Adleman (RSA): An asymmetric encryption algorithm used for secure key exchange, digital signatures, and encryption. RSA relies on the difficulty of factoring large prime numbers for its security.
c. Elliptic Curve Cryptography (ECC): An asymmetric encryption scheme based on elliptic curves, offering strong security with shorter key lengths compared to RSA, making it suitable for resource-constrained environments and cryptographic operations.
d. Hashing Algorithms: Secure Hash Algorithm (SHA) family (e.g., SHA-256, SHA-3), Message Digest Algorithm (MD5), and cryptographic hash functions used for data integrity, digital signatures, and password hashing.

4. Cryptographic Applications:
a. Secure Communication: Encryption protocols such as TLS/SSL, IPSec, and SSH use cryptographic algorithms for secure data transmission, virtual private networking (VPN), and secure remote access.
b. Data Protection: Encrypting sensitive data at rest (stored data encryption) and in transit (network encryption) protects against unauthorized access, data breaches, and eavesdropping.

c. Digital Signatures: Verifying the authenticity and integrity of digital documents, emails, software updates, and electronic transactions using digital signatures and public-key cryptography.

d. Blockchain Technology: Utilizing cryptographic hashing, digital signatures, and consensus algorithms in blockchain networks for secure, tamper-proof distributed ledger technology (DLT) applications, such as cryptocurrencies (e.g., Bitcoin, Ethereum) and smart contracts.

5. Cryptographic Security Considerations:

a. Key Management: Secure generation, storage, distribution, and rotation of cryptographic keys, ensuring key confidentiality, integrity, and availability.

b. Cryptographic Strength: Evaluating encryption algorithms, key lengths, and cryptographic implementations to withstand brute-force attacks, cryptographic attacks, and advances in computing technologies (e.g., quantum computing).

c. Cryptographic Protocols: Implementing secure cryptographic protocols, standards, and best practices (e.g., PKI, HMAC, digital certificates) for secure authentication, data integrity, and secure communication over networks.

d. Cryptographic Lifecycle Management: Establishing policies, procedures, and controls for cryptographic key lifecycle management, key usage policies, key escrow, and secure key disposal to maintain cryptographic security over time.

Conclusion:

Cryptography plays a vital role in securing digital assets, ensuring privacy, enabling secure communication, and building trust in digital transactions and systems. Understanding cryptographic principles, encryption algorithms, key management practices, and cryptographic security considerations is essential for cybersecurity professionals, developers, and organizations to implement robust cryptographic solutions, protect sensitive data, and mitigate cyber threats in today's dynamic and interconnected cyber landscape. Continuous research, adherence to cryptographic standards, and staying informed about emerging cryptographic technologies and threats are key to maintaining strong cryptographic security posture and data protection capabilities.

Chapter: Information Security

Information security is paramount in safeguarding sensitive data, ensuring business continuity, and protecting digital assets against cyber threats and unauthorized access. This chapter delves into the principles of information security, security frameworks, risk management practices, and strategies for establishing a robust information security posture.

1. Understanding Information Security:
Information security (InfoSec) encompasses policies, procedures, technologies, and practices designed to protect information assets (data, systems, networks) from unauthorized access, disclosure, alteration, disruption, or destruction. It aims to ensure confidentiality, integrity, availability (CIA triad), authenticity, and non-repudiation of data and systems.

2. Information Security Principles:
a. Confidentiality: Ensuring that sensitive information is accessible only to authorized users, preventing unauthorized disclosure or access.
b. Integrity: Maintaining the accuracy, consistency, and trustworthiness of data and systems, protecting against unauthorized modifications or tampering.
c. Availability: Ensuring timely and reliable access to information and resources when needed by authorized users, preventing disruptions or downtime.
d. Authenticity: Verifying the identity of users, systems, and data sources to ensure trustworthiness and prevent impersonation or unauthorized access.

e. Non-repudiation: Providing proof of origin or delivery of data, transactions, or communications to prevent denial of involvement or responsibility.

3. Information Security Components:
a. Access Control: Implementing authentication mechanisms (e.g., passwords, biometrics, tokens) and authorization controls (e.g., role-based access control) to enforce least privilege access and protect against unauthorized access.
b. Encryption: Using strong encryption algorithms (e.g., AES, RSA) to protect data confidentiality at rest and in transit, securing sensitive information from unauthorized disclosure.
c. Firewalls and Intrusion Detection/Prevention Systems (IDS/IPS): Deploying network firewalls and monitoring systems to detect and block malicious traffic, intrusions, and cyber attacks targeting networks and systems.
d. Security Policies and Procedures: Establishing and enforcing information security policies, standards, guidelines, and procedures governing data protection, access controls, incident response, and compliance requirements.
e. Security Awareness and Training: Educating employees, users, and stakeholders about information security risks, best practices, phishing prevention, and incident reporting to enhance security awareness and resilience.

4. Information Security Frameworks and Standards:
a. ISO/IEC 27001: International standard for information security management systems (ISMS), providing a risk-based framework for identifying, assessing, and mitigating information security risks and establishing security controls.
b. NIST Cybersecurity Framework: Framework developed by the National Institute of Standards and Technology (NIST) to improve cybersecurity risk management across critical infrastructure sectors, emphasizing risk management, security controls, and incident response.

c. GDPR and Privacy Regulations: Compliance with General Data Protection Regulation (GDPR), data protection laws, and privacy regulations governing data collection, processing, storage, and transfer, ensuring data privacy and rights of individuals.

d. PCI DSS: Payment Card Industry Data Security Standard outlines security requirements for organizations handling payment card data to prevent payment fraud, data breaches, and secure payment transactions.

5. Risk Management and Incident Response:

a. Risk Assessment: Identifying, analyzing, and prioritizing information security risks (e.g., threats, vulnerabilities, impact) to determine risk levels and mitigation strategies.

b. Security Controls: Implementing administrative, technical, and physical security controls (e.g., access controls, encryption, patch management) to mitigate identified risks and protect information assets.

c. Incident Response: Developing and implementing incident response plans, procedures, and teams to detect, respond to, contain, and recover from security incidents, data breaches, and cyber attacks promptly.

d. Continuous Monitoring and Improvement: Monitoring security controls, threat intelligence, security events, and compliance metrics regularly to detect anomalies, assess security posture, and improve information security practices continuously.

Conclusion:

Information security is a strategic imperative for organizations and individuals to protect sensitive data, maintain business continuity, comply with regulations, and build trust with stakeholders. By adopting information security principles, implementing robust security controls, leveraging security frameworks, conducting risk assessments, providing security training, and establishing incident response capabilities, organizations can enhance their information security posture, resilience against cyber threats, and maintain a secure digital environment in today's evolving threat landscape. Collaboration, awareness, and a proactive approach to information security are key to mitigating risks, protecting critical assets, and ensuring a secure and trusted information ecosystem.

Chapter: Information Security

Information security plays a crucial role in safeguarding data, systems, and networks from unauthorized access, breaches, and cyber threats. This chapter delves into the core concepts of information security, key principles, security measures, and strategies for implementing effective information security practices.

1. Understanding Information Security:
Information security is a discipline focused on protecting information assets from unauthorized access, use, disclosure, disruption, modification, or destruction. It encompasses technical, administrative, and physical controls designed to ensure confidentiality, integrity, and availability (CIA) of data and systems.

2. Core Principles of Information Security:
a. Confidentiality: Ensuring that sensitive information is accessible only to authorized individuals or entities, preventing unauthorized disclosure or access.
b. Integrity: Maintaining the accuracy, reliability, and trustworthiness of data and systems, ensuring that data remains unaltered and reliable.
c. Availability: Ensuring that information and systems are available and accessible to authorized users when needed, minimizing downtime and disruptions.
d. Authenticity: Verifying the identity of users, systems, and data to ensure that they are genuine and trustworthy, preventing unauthorized impersonation or access.
e. Non-repudiation: Providing proof of the origin or delivery of data, transactions, or communications, ensuring that parties cannot deny their actions or involvement.

3. Components of Information Security:
a. Access Control: Implementing mechanisms such as authentication, authorization, and accountability to control access to systems, applications, and data based on user roles and permissions.
b. Data Encryption: Using cryptographic techniques to convert plaintext data into ciphertext, protecting data confidentiality during storage, transmission, and processing.
c. Security Policies and Procedures: Establishing and enforcing policies, standards, guidelines, and procedures related to information security, data handling, access control, and incident response.
d. Security Awareness and Training: Educating employees, users, and stakeholders about security risks, best practices, policies, and procedures to promote a security-conscious culture and behavior.
e. Security Monitoring and Incident Response: Implementing monitoring tools, intrusion detection systems (IDS), security information and event management (SIEM) solutions, and incident response plans to detect, respond to, and mitigate security incidents and breaches.

4. Security Measures and Technologies:
a. Firewalls and Intrusion Detection/Prevention Systems (IDS/IPS): Deploying network firewalls, IDS, and IPS solutions to monitor and control incoming and outgoing network traffic, detect suspicious activities, and prevent unauthorized access or attacks.
b. Vulnerability Management: Conducting regular vulnerability assessments, scans, and patch management to identify and mitigate security vulnerabilities in systems, applications, and devices.
c. Encryption Technologies: Implementing encryption algorithms (e.g., AES, RSA) for data-at-rest encryption, data-in-transit encryption (e.g., SSL/TLS), and securing communication channels and sensitive data.

d. Multi-factor Authentication (MFA): Enhancing authentication security by requiring multiple factors (e.g., passwords, biometrics, tokens) for user authentication, reducing the risk of unauthorized access due to compromised credentials.

e. Security Audits and Compliance: Performing regular security audits, assessments, and compliance checks against security standards, regulations (e.g., GDPR, PCI DSS), and industry best practices to ensure adherence to security requirements and mitigate risks.

5. Information Security Frameworks and Standards:

a. ISO/IEC 27001: International standard for Information Security Management Systems (ISMS), providing a framework for implementing, maintaining, and improving information security controls and practices.

b. NIST Cybersecurity Framework: Framework developed by the National Institute of Standards and Technology (NIST) to guide organizations in managing and reducing cybersecurity risks, improving security posture, and enhancing resilience.

c. PCI DSS: Payment Card Industry Data Security Standard for organizations handling payment card information, outlining security requirements, controls, and practices to protect cardholder data and prevent payment fraud.

d. GDPR and Privacy Regulations: Compliance with General Data Protection Regulation (GDPR), data protection laws, and privacy regulations governing the collection, processing, storage, and sharing of personal data, ensuring data privacy rights and security.

6. Challenges and Emerging Trends:

a. Cyber Threat Landscape: Evolving cyber threats such as ransomware, phishing, insider threats, and advanced persistent threats (APTs) require continuous monitoring, threat intelligence, and adaptive security measures.

b. Cloud Security: Securing cloud environments, services, and data with robust access controls, encryption, identity management, and security monitoring in cloud-native and hybrid cloud architectures.

c. IoT Security: Addressing security challenges in Internet of Things (IoT) devices, networks, and ecosystems, including device authentication, data encryption, firmware updates, and IoT security standards.

d. AI and Machine Learning in Security: Leveraging AI-driven analytics, machine learning algorithms, and automation for threat detection, anomaly detection, behavioral analysis, and security incident response.

e. Privacy and Data Protection: Ensuring data privacy, transparency, consent management, and compliance with privacy regulations amid increasing data breaches, data sharing, and data-driven technologies.

Conclusion:
Information security is a multidimensional discipline encompassing technological, organizational, and human factors to protect data, systems, and networks from cyber threats and vulnerabilities. By adopting a risk-based approach, implementing security measures and technologies, fostering security awareness, and complying with security standards and regulations, organizations can enhance their information security posture, reduce risks, and maintain trust with stakeholders in an evolving digital landscape. Continuous monitoring, threat intelligence sharing, incident response readiness, and collaboration across teams are essential for addressing emerging threats, adapting to technological advancements, and ensuring effective information security governance and resilience.

Chapter: Secure Communication

Secure communication is paramount in today's digital age to protect sensitive information, maintain privacy, and ensure data integrity during data transmission across networks. This chapter explores the principles of secure communication, encryption technologies, secure protocols, and best practices for establishing and maintaining secure communication channels.

1. Principles of Secure Communication:
Secure communication aims to protect data confidentiality, integrity, authenticity, and availability during transmission over insecure networks such as the internet or public networks. The following principles guide secure communication:

Confidentiality: Ensuring that data remains private and accessible only to authorized recipients.
Integrity: Verifying that data remains unchanged and unaltered during transmission, preventing unauthorized modifications or tampering.
Authentication: Verifying the identities of communicating parties to ensure trustworthiness and prevent impersonation or unauthorized access.
Non-repudiation: Providing proof of origin or delivery of data, transactions, or communications to prevent denial of involvement or responsibility.
2. Encryption Technologies:
Encryption plays a vital role in securing communication channels by converting plaintext data into ciphertext, which can only be decrypted by authorized parties possessing the decryption keys. Common encryption technologies include:

Symmetric Encryption: Uses a single shared key for encryption and decryption (e.g., AES, DES, 3DES), suitable for fast and efficient encryption of data.

Asymmetric Encryption: Utilizes public-private key pairs for encryption and decryption (e.g., RSA, ECC), enabling secure key exchange, digital signatures, and secure communication channels.

3. Secure Communication Protocols:

Secure communication protocols incorporate encryption, authentication, and integrity mechanisms to establish secure communication channels between parties. Common secure protocols include:

Transport Layer Security (TLS) / Secure Sockets Layer (SSL): Protocols used for securing web communications (HTTPS), email transmissions (SMTPS, IMAPS), and other network protocols with encryption, mutual authentication, and data integrity checks.

Internet Protocol Security (IPsec): Protocol suite for securing IP communications by encrypting and authenticating IP packets, commonly used in VPNs for secure remote access and site-to-site connections.

Secure File Transfer Protocols: Protocols like SFTP (SSH File Transfer Protocol), FTPS (FTP over SSL/TLS), and AS2 (Applicability Statement 2) for secure file transfers with encryption, authentication, and data integrity.

4. Best Practices for Secure Communication:

a. Use Strong Encryption: Implement encryption algorithms with strong key lengths and secure encryption protocols (e.g., AES-256, RSA-2048) for data protection.

b. Enable Secure Protocols: Use secure communication protocols (e.g., TLS/SSL) for web, email, and network communications to prevent eavesdropping and data interception.

c. Implement Authentication: Use strong authentication mechanisms (e.g., passwords, biometrics, tokens) and mutual authentication in secure protocols to verify identities and prevent unauthorized access.

d. Regularly Update and Patch: Keep software, applications, and encryption libraries up to date with security patches and updates to address vulnerabilities and weaknesses.

e. Use VPNs for Remote Access: Implement Virtual Private Networks (VPNs) with IPsec or SSL VPNs for secure remote access to corporate networks, ensuring encrypted and authenticated connections.

f. Encrypt Sensitive Data: Encrypt sensitive data at rest and in transit using encryption technologies to protect confidentiality and data integrity.

g. Monitor and Audit: Implement logging, monitoring, and auditing mechanisms to track and analyze security events, detect anomalies, and ensure compliance with security policies.

5. Future Trends in Secure Communication:

a. Post-Quantum Cryptography: Exploring quantum-resistant encryption algorithms and protocols to prepare for the potential threat of quantum computing on current encryption standards.

b. Homomorphic Encryption: Advancing encryption techniques that allow computation on encrypted data without decryption, preserving data privacy in cloud computing and data analytics.

c. Secure IoT Communication: Developing secure communication protocols, encryption standards, and authentication mechanisms for Internet of Things (IoT) devices and ecosystems to mitigate IoT security risks.

d. Blockchain-Based Communication: Leveraging blockchain technology for secure, decentralized communication channels, smart contracts, and digital identities, enhancing trust and security in peer-to-peer transactions and communications.

Conclusion:

Secure communication is essential for protecting sensitive information, ensuring data privacy, and maintaining trust in digital interactions and transactions. By understanding encryption technologies, implementing secure communication protocols, following best practices, and embracing emerging security trends, organizations can establish robust secure communication channels, mitigate cybersecurity risks, and safeguard critical data and communications in today's interconnected world. Continuous education, monitoring, and adaptation to evolving threats and technologies are key to maintaining effective secure communication strategies and resilience against cyber threats.

Chapter: Encryption Techniques

Encryption serves as a cornerstone of modern cybersecurity, ensuring the confidentiality and integrity of sensitive information during storage, transmission, and processing. This chapter explores various encryption techniques, encryption algorithms, key management, and their applications in securing data across different environments.

1. Symmetric Encryption:
Symmetric encryption uses a single shared key for both encryption and decryption processes. It is computationally efficient for bulk data encryption and commonly used for securing data at rest.

AES (Advanced Encryption Standard): Widely adopted symmetric encryption algorithm known for its security, speed, and versatility. AES supports key lengths of 128, 192, and 256 bits, providing strong encryption for sensitive data.
2. Asymmetric Encryption:
Asymmetric encryption (public-key cryptography) uses a pair of keys - public and private keys - for encryption and decryption. It facilitates secure key exchange, digital signatures, and secure communication channels.

RSA (Rivest-Shamir-Adleman): Popular asymmetric encryption algorithm used for secure communication, key exchange, and digital signatures. RSA's security relies on the difficulty of factoring large prime numbers.
ECC (Elliptic Curve Cryptography): Offers strong security with shorter key lengths compared to RSA, making it suitable for resource-constrained environments and cryptographic operations in IoT devices and mobile platforms.
3. Hashing Algorithms:

Hashing algorithms generate fixed-length hash values (hash codes) from input data, ensuring data integrity, and providing a unique identifier for data.

SHA-256 (Secure Hash Algorithm-256): Part of the SHA-2 family, SHA-256 generates a 256-bit hash value, commonly used for data integrity verification, digital signatures, and password hashing.
MD5 (Message Digest Algorithm 5): Despite being less secure due to vulnerabilities, MD5 is still used for checksums, fingerprinting, and non-cryptographic applications.
4. Hybrid Encryption:
Hybrid encryption combines symmetric and asymmetric encryption techniques to leverage their strengths for efficient and secure data protection.

Key Exchange: Asymmetric encryption is used for secure key exchange, encrypting the symmetric key used for bulk data encryption.
Bulk Data Encryption: Symmetric encryption is employed for encrypting data with the shared symmetric key, ensuring fast and efficient encryption and decryption operations.
5. Key Management:
Effective key management is crucial for maintaining the security of encrypted data and communication channels.

Key Generation: Secure generation of cryptographic keys using strong random number generators (RNGs) or hardware security modules (HSMs).
Key Storage: Secure storage of encryption keys, separating keys from encrypted data, and utilizing key vaults or secure storage solutions.
Key Rotation: Regularly updating and rotating encryption keys to mitigate risks associated with key compromise or exposure.

Key Distribution: Secure distribution of encryption keys using key exchange protocols (e.g., Diffie-Hellman) or key management systems (KMS).

6. Applications of Encryption:

Encryption techniques find widespread applications in various domains to protect data and communications.

Data Encryption: Securing sensitive data at rest (disk encryption, database encryption) and in transit (SSL/TLS encryption, VPNs) to prevent unauthorized access and data breaches.

Email Encryption: Encrypting email communications (PGP, S/MIME) to protect sensitive information and ensure confidentiality.

Secure File Transfer: Using encrypted protocols (SFTP, FTPS) for secure file transfers, ensuring data integrity and confidentiality.

Cloud Security: Encrypting data stored in the cloud (client-side encryption, encryption at rest) and securing communication channels (TLS/SSL) in cloud environments.

Conclusion:

Encryption techniques play a vital role in securing data, communications, and digital transactions, ensuring confidentiality, integrity, and authenticity in today's interconnected and data-driven environments. Understanding the strengths and limitations of symmetric encryption, asymmetric encryption, hashing algorithms, and key management practices is essential for implementing robust encryption strategies, mitigating security risks, and safeguarding sensitive information against cyber threats and data breaches. Continuous evaluation of encryption technologies, adherence to encryption standards, and proactive key management practices are key elements of a comprehensive encryption strategy in modern cybersecurity frameworks.

Chapter: Encryption Protocols

Encryption protocols form the backbone of secure communication over networks, ensuring data confidentiality, integrity, and authentication. This chapter explores prominent encryption protocols used in securing various communication channels and data transmissions.

1. Transport Layer Security (TLS) / Secure Sockets Layer (SSL):
TLS and its predecessor SSL are cryptographic protocols designed to secure communication over networks like the internet. They establish encrypted connections between clients and servers, protecting data during transmission.

Encryption Algorithms: TLS/SSL support various encryption algorithms (e.g., AES, RSA, ECC) for data encryption, ensuring confidentiality.
Handshake Protocol: TLS/SSL handshakes establish a secure connection, negotiate encryption parameters, and authenticate parties using digital certificates.
Versions: Different versions of TLS/SSL (e.g., TLS 1.2, TLS 1.3) offer improved security features, cipher suites, and protocols for secure communication.
2. IPsec (Internet Protocol Security):
IPsec is a suite of protocols used to secure IP communications by authenticating and encrypting IP packets. It is commonly used in virtual private networks (VPNs) for secure remote access and site-to-site connections.

Security Associations (SAs): IPsec establishes SAs between communicating nodes, defining security parameters such as encryption algorithms, authentication methods, and key exchange protocols.

Modes: IPsec supports transport mode (protects data payload) and tunnel mode (protects entire IP packet), providing flexibility in securing different network architectures.

3. Pretty Good Privacy (PGP) / GNU Privacy Guard (GPG):
PGP and GPG are asymmetric encryption protocols used for securing email communications, file encryption, and digital signatures.

Encryption: PGP/GPG use a combination of symmetric and asymmetric encryption for secure email encryption and decryption.

Key Management: PGP/GPG employ key pairs (public and private keys) for encryption, digital signatures, and key exchange, ensuring secure communication channels.

4. Secure Shell (SSH):
SSH is a secure protocol for remote access, file transfer, and secure communication between networked devices. It provides encryption, authentication, and data integrity checks for secure command-line access and file transfers (SCP, SFTP).

Authentication: SSH supports various authentication methods (passwords, public key, multi-factor authentication) for secure user access to remote systems.

Encryption: SSH encrypts data transmissions (including commands, files) between SSH client and server, protecting against eavesdropping and tampering.

5. Secure File Transfer Protocols:
Secure file transfer protocols such as SFTP (SSH File Transfer Protocol) and FTPS (FTP over SSL/TLS) ensure secure data transfer over networks, protecting file integrity and confidentiality.

SFTP: Uses SSH for secure file transfers, providing encryption, authentication, and data integrity checks.

FTPS: Utilizes TLS/SSL for FTP sessions, encrypting control and data channels for secure file transfers.

6. HTTPS (Hypertext Transfer Protocol Secure):
HTTPS is an extension of HTTP with added security features provided by TLS/SSL encryption. It secures web communication, online transactions, and sensitive data exchanges on websites.

SSL/TLS Certificates: Websites use SSL/TLS certificates to enable HTTPS, verify website authenticity, and encrypt data exchanged between clients (web browsers) and servers.
Padlock Icon: Browsers indicate secure HTTPS connections with a padlock icon, assuring users of encrypted and authenticated web sessions.

Conclusion:
Encryption protocols play a vital role in ensuring secure communication, data protection, and privacy across networks and digital environments. Understanding and implementing appropriate encryption protocols such as TLS/SSL, IPsec, PGP/GPG, SSH, and secure file transfer protocols are crucial steps in safeguarding sensitive information, mitigating cybersecurity risks, and maintaining trust in digital interactions. Continuous updates, adherence to encryption standards, secure key management practices, and monitoring encryption implementations are essential for maintaining robust encryption protocols in modern cybersecurity architectures.

Chapter: Encryption Standards

Encryption standards form the foundation of secure communication, data protection, and cryptographic operations across various industries and applications. This chapter explores prominent encryption standards, their significance, key features, and their impact on cybersecurity practices.

1. Advanced Encryption Standard (AES):
AES is a symmetric encryption standard widely adopted for securing sensitive data in various applications, including data-at-rest encryption, network encryption, and secure communication protocols like TLS/SSL.

Key Lengths: AES supports key lengths of 128, 192, and 256 bits, offering strong encryption capabilities and resistance against brute-force attacks.
Efficiency: AES is computationally efficient, making it suitable for resource-constrained devices and high-speed encryption/decryption operations.
2. RSA (Rivest-Shamir-Adleman):
RSA is an asymmetric encryption standard used for secure key exchange, digital signatures, and encryption in secure communication protocols like TLS/SSL.

Public-Key Cryptography: RSA employs public-key cryptography, utilizing public and private key pairs for encryption and decryption operations.
Key Sizes: RSA supports key sizes ranging from 1024 bits to 4096 bits, with larger key sizes offering higher security but requiring more computational resources.
3. Elliptic Curve Cryptography (ECC):

ECC is an asymmetric encryption standard known for its strong security with shorter key lengths compared to RSA, making it ideal for resource-constrained devices and cryptographic operations in IoT and mobile environments.

Key Lengths: ECC key lengths are shorter than RSA for equivalent security levels, reducing computational overhead and storage requirements.
Security: ECC offers robust security against attacks like brute-force and factorization due to the mathematical properties of elliptic curves.

4. Secure Hash Algorithms (SHA):
SHA family of cryptographic hash functions, including SHA-1, SHA-2, and SHA-3, are widely used for data integrity verification, digital signatures, and password hashing.

SHA-256: Part of the SHA-2 family, SHA-256 generates a 256-bit hash value, offering stronger security and collision resistance compared to SHA-1.
SHA-3: The latest addition to the SHA family, SHA-3 utilizes a different internal structure (Keccak) and offers enhanced security properties, making it resistant to certain cryptographic attacks.

5. Key Management Standards:
Effective key management is crucial for maintaining the security of encryption keys used in cryptographic operations. Key management standards and protocols include:

Key Management Interoperability Protocol (KMIP): Industry-standard protocol for managing encryption keys and cryptographic objects across diverse cryptographic systems and platforms.
Public Key Infrastructure (PKI): Framework consisting of hardware, software, policies, and procedures for managing digital certificates, public-private key pairs, and secure communication.

X.509 Certificates: Standard format for public-key certificates used in SSL/TLS, digital signatures, and authentication, following the X.509 standard defined by the International Telecommunication Union (ITU).

6. Compliance and Regulatory Standards:

Several compliance and regulatory standards mandate the use of specific encryption standards and practices to protect sensitive data, ensure privacy, and mitigate cybersecurity risks:

PCI DSS (Payment Card Industry Data Security Standard): Requires strong encryption (e.g., AES-256) for protecting payment card data during transmission and storage.

HIPAA (Health Insurance Portability and Accountability Act): Mandates encryption of electronic protected health information (ePHI) to ensure patient data confidentiality and security.

GDPR (General Data Protection Regulation): Requires encryption and pseudonymization of personal data to protect data subjects' privacy and prevent unauthorized access.

Conclusion:

Encryption standards play a critical role in ensuring data confidentiality, integrity, and authenticity in modern cybersecurity practices. Adherence to established encryption standards such as AES, RSA, ECC, and SHA, along with robust key management practices and compliance with regulatory standards, is essential for organizations to safeguard sensitive information, protect against cyber threats, and maintain trust with stakeholders in today's digital landscape. Continuous monitoring of encryption technologies, updates to cryptographic protocols, and adherence to best practices are key elements of a comprehensive encryption strategy in cybersecurity frameworks.

Chapter: Symmetric Encryption

Symmetric encryption is a fundamental cryptographic technique used to secure data by using a single shared key for both encryption and decryption processes. This chapter explores the principles, algorithms, modes, and applications of symmetric encryption in modern cybersecurity.

1. Principles of Symmetric Encryption:
Symmetric encryption follows the principle of using the same secret key for both encryption and decryption operations. This key must be kept confidential between communicating parties to maintain data security.

2. Symmetric Encryption Algorithms:
Several symmetric encryption algorithms are widely used to encrypt data securely. Some prominent algorithms include:

Advanced Encryption Standard (AES): A block cipher algorithm adopted as the encryption standard by the U.S. government. AES supports key lengths of 128, 192, and 256 bits and is highly secure and efficient.
Data Encryption Standard (DES): An older symmetric encryption algorithm using a 56-bit key. While DES is no longer recommended for sensitive data due to its small key size, Triple DES (3DES) enhances security by applying DES encryption three times sequentially.
3. Modes of Operation:
Symmetric encryption algorithms operate in different modes to provide confidentiality, integrity, and authenticity to encrypted data. Common modes include:

Electronic Codebook (ECB): Divides data into blocks and encrypts each block separately. Identical plaintext blocks encrypt to the same ciphertext block, which can lead to security vulnerabilities in some scenarios.

Cipher Block Chaining (CBC): XORs each plaintext block with the previous ciphertext block before encryption, introducing randomness and preventing identical blocks from encrypting to the same ciphertext.

Cipher Feedback (CFB) and Output Feedback (OFB): Modes that turn block ciphers into stream ciphers, encrypting individual bits or bytes of data. They are suited for encrypting streaming data or communication channels.

4. Key Management in Symmetric Encryption:

Managing symmetric encryption keys securely is crucial to maintaining data confidentiality. Key management practices include:

Key Generation: Using secure random number generators (RNGs) to create strong keys with sufficient entropy.

Key Distribution: Securely sharing keys between authorized parties using key exchange protocols (e.g., Diffie-Hellman) or key management systems.

Key Rotation: Periodically changing encryption keys to limit exposure in case of key compromise.

5. Applications of Symmetric Encryption:

Symmetric encryption finds widespread applications in securing data at rest, data in transit, and communication channels:

Data Encryption: Encrypting files, databases, and storage devices to protect sensitive information from unauthorized access or theft.

Secure Communication: Securing network communications, VPN tunnels, and encrypted protocols (e.g., TLS/SSL) for secure data transmission over the internet.

Authentication: Symmetric encryption is also used in message authentication codes (MACs) and hash-based message authentication codes (HMACs) to verify data integrity and authenticity.

6. Symmetric Encryption Best Practices:

Use Strong Keys: Choose encryption keys with sufficient length (e.g., 256 bits for AES) to resist brute-force attacks.
Secure Key Storage: Store encryption keys securely using hardware security modules (HSMs), key management systems (KMS), or secure key vaults.
Key Lifecycle Management: Implement key rotation, revocation, and destruction policies to manage keys throughout their lifecycle securely.
Encryption Performance: Consider encryption/decryption performance overheads for large-scale deployments and optimize cryptographic operations as needed.

Conclusion:

Symmetric encryption is a cornerstone of modern cryptography, providing efficient and secure data protection for a wide range of applications. Understanding symmetric encryption principles, algorithms, modes, key management practices, and best practices is essential for implementing robust encryption solutions, mitigating cybersecurity risks, and safeguarding sensitive information in today's digital environments. Continuous evaluation of encryption technologies and adherence to industry standards contribute to maintaining strong data security postures and ensuring trust in data confidentiality and integrity.

Chapter: Asymmetric Encryption

Asymmetric encryption, also known as public-key cryptography, revolutionized secure communication by introducing a pair of keys for encryption and decryption processes. This chapter delves into the principles, algorithms, key management, and applications of asymmetric encryption in modern cybersecurity.

1. Principles of Asymmetric Encryption:
Asymmetric encryption uses a pair of mathematically related keys - a public key and a private key. The public key is widely distributed and used for encryption, while the private key is kept secret and used for decryption. This asymmetry allows secure communication between parties without the need to exchange secret keys.

2. Asymmetric Encryption Algorithms:
Several asymmetric encryption algorithms are widely used in secure communication and digital signatures:

RSA (Rivest-Shamir-Adleman): A popular asymmetric encryption algorithm for secure key exchange, encryption, and digital signatures. RSA relies on the difficulty of factoring large prime numbers for security.
Elliptic Curve Cryptography (ECC): Utilizes elliptic curves over finite fields to create smaller key sizes with equivalent security levels compared to RSA, making it ideal for resource-constrained environments like IoT devices and mobile platforms.
3. Key Pair Generation and Usage:

Key Pair Generation: Users generate a public-private key pair using cryptographic algorithms. The public key is shared openly, while the private key remains confidential.

Encryption: Data encrypted with the recipient's public key can only be decrypted by the corresponding private key, ensuring confidentiality during transmission.

Digital Signatures: Using the sender's private key to create a digital signature ensures data integrity, authenticity, and non-repudiation. The recipient can verify the signature using the sender's public key.

4. Applications of Asymmetric Encryption:

Asymmetric encryption is integral to various security applications and protocols:

Secure Communication: Establishing secure communication channels, key exchange, and encrypted sessions in protocols like TLS/SSL, SSH, and HTTPS.

Digital Signatures: Verifying document authenticity, ensuring data integrity, and enabling non-repudiation in electronic transactions and communications.

Key Management: Securely exchanging symmetric encryption keys (session keys) using asymmetric encryption during initial communication setup.

5. Hybrid Cryptography:

Hybrid cryptography combines symmetric and asymmetric encryption techniques to leverage their strengths:

Key Exchange: Asymmetric encryption is used for secure key exchange, encrypting symmetric session keys used for bulk data encryption.

Bulk Data Encryption: Symmetric encryption is employed for encrypting actual data, offering efficiency and speed for large volumes of data.

6. Asymmetric Encryption Best Practices:

Key Lengths: Use recommended key lengths (e.g., 2048 bits for RSA, elliptic curve parameters) to ensure sufficient security against modern cryptographic attacks.

Key Management: Protect private keys with strong access controls, encryption, and secure storage mechanisms (e.g., hardware security modules - HSMs).

Certificate Authorities (CAs): Implement proper trust and validation mechanisms for public keys using trusted certificate authorities for digital certificates.

Performance Considerations: Balance security requirements with performance considerations in asymmetric encryption operations, optimizing cryptographic operations as needed.

Conclusion:

Asymmetric encryption has revolutionized secure communication, digital signatures, and key management in cybersecurity. Understanding the principles, algorithms, key management practices, and applications of asymmetric encryption is crucial for designing robust encryption solutions, securing sensitive data, and maintaining trust in digital interactions. Continuous evaluation of encryption technologies, adherence to key management best practices, and compliance with encryption standards contribute to a strong security posture and effective data protection strategies in modern cybersecurity landscapes.

Chapter: Encryption Keys

Encryption keys are fundamental components of cryptographic systems, enabling secure data encryption, decryption, and communication. This chapter explores the types of encryption keys, key generation techniques, key management practices, and the importance of secure key handling in modern cybersecurity.

1. Types of Encryption Keys:
Encryption keys can be classified based on their usage and generation methods:

Symmetric Keys: Used in symmetric encryption algorithms where the same key is used for both encryption and decryption processes. Symmetric keys require secure key distribution mechanisms.
Asymmetric Key Pairs: Consist of a public key and a corresponding private key used in asymmetric encryption (public-key cryptography). Public keys are openly shared, while private keys are kept secret.
2. Key Generation Techniques:
Secure key generation is crucial to ensure the strength and randomness of encryption keys:

Pseudorandom Number Generators (PRNGs): Algorithms used to generate keys based on initial seed values, producing sequences of seemingly random numbers suitable for encryption keys.

True Random Number Generators (TRNGs): Utilize physical processes (e.g., electronic noise, radioactive decay) to generate truly random numbers, enhancing key randomness and security.

3. Key Length and Strength:

The length of encryption keys directly impacts their strength and resistance to cryptographic attacks:

Symmetric Keys: Longer key lengths (e.g., 256 bits for AES) increase key space and computational complexity, enhancing security against brute-force attacks.

Asymmetric Keys: Recommended key lengths (e.g., 2048 bits for RSA) ensure sufficient security against factorization and cryptographic attacks.

4. Key Management Practices:

Effective key management is essential to maintain the security and confidentiality of encryption keys:

Key Generation: Use secure and trusted algorithms for key generation, ensuring randomness and strength.

Key Distribution: Securely distribute symmetric keys using key exchange protocols (e.g., Diffie-Hellman) or key management systems (KMS). Protect private keys in asymmetric key pairs.

Key Storage: Store encryption keys securely using hardware security modules (HSMs), key vaults, or encrypted storage solutions to prevent unauthorized access.

Key Rotation: Regularly update and rotate encryption keys to limit exposure in case of key compromise or cryptographic vulnerabilities.

5. Importance of Secure Key Handling:

Confidentiality: Secure key handling practices prevent unauthorized access and disclosure of encryption keys, ensuring data confidentiality.

Integrity: Protecting keys from tampering or modification maintains the integrity of encryption processes and prevents unauthorized decryption.

Availability: Ensuring access to encryption keys when needed while preventing unauthorized or accidental key deletion or loss.

Compliance: Adhering to key management best practices and compliance requirements (e.g., PCI DSS, GDPR) for data protection and security standards.

6. Key Escrow and Recovery:

In scenarios where key loss or compromise may occur, key escrow and recovery mechanisms can be implemented to recover encrypted data or regenerate lost keys securely.

Conclusion:

Encryption keys are foundational elements in cryptography, ensuring data confidentiality, integrity, and security in digital communications and data protection. Understanding key types, generation techniques, key management practices, and secure key handling is crucial for designing robust encryption systems, mitigating cryptographic risks, and maintaining trust in secure data transactions and communications. Continuous monitoring, key lifecycle management, and compliance with encryption standards contribute to a strong security posture and effective data protection strategies in cybersecurity frameworks.

Chapter: Key Management

Key management is a critical aspect of cryptographic systems that involves the secure generation, distribution, storage, rotation, and disposal of encryption keys. This chapter explores key management principles, key lifecycle stages, best practices, and the importance of secure key management in ensuring data confidentiality and integrity in modern cybersecurity.

1. Key Lifecycle Stages:
Key management encompasses several key lifecycle stages, each crucial for maintaining the security of encryption keys:

Key Generation: Securely creating encryption keys using trusted algorithms and random number generators (RNGs) to ensure randomness and strength.

Key Distribution: Safely sharing symmetric keys or distributing public keys in asymmetric key pairs to authorized entities using secure channels or protocols.

Key Usage: Employing keys for encryption, decryption, digital signatures, and secure communication as per cryptographic requirements.

Key Storage: Securely storing encryption keys using hardware security modules (HSMs), key management systems (KMS), or encrypted storage solutions to prevent unauthorized access or theft.

Key Rotation: Regularly updating and rotating encryption keys to limit exposure in case of key compromise or vulnerabilities.

Key Retirement and Disposal: Securely decommissioning and disposing of encryption keys no longer in use, ensuring they cannot be recovered or reused.

2. Key Management Best Practices:

Implementing key management best practices is crucial to maintain the security and integrity of encryption keys throughout their lifecycle:

Use Strong Key Generation: Generate keys with sufficient length and randomness using cryptographic standards and secure algorithms (e.g., AES-256, RSA-2048).

Secure Key Storage: Store encryption keys in secure environments such as hardware security modules (HSMs) or secure key vaults with access controls, encryption, and auditing capabilities.

Key Access Control: Implement strict access controls and least privilege principles to restrict key access to authorized personnel or systems based on roles and responsibilities.

Key Rotation and Refresh: Regularly rotate encryption keys and refresh cryptographic materials (e.g., certificates) to reduce the risk of key compromise and cryptographic attacks.

Monitoring and Auditing: Continuously monitor key usage, access logs, and key management activities to detect unauthorized access attempts, anomalies, or security incidents.

Compliance and Standards: Adhere to industry standards (e.g., NIST SP 800-57, PCI DSS, GDPR) and regulatory requirements for key management practices, data protection, and security controls.

3. Key Management Systems (KMS):

Key management systems provide centralized management, automation, and security controls for encryption keys across diverse environments and cryptographic applications:

Centralized Key Storage: Securely store and manage encryption keys, digital certificates, and cryptographic materials in a centralized repository.

Key Lifecycle Management: Automate key generation, distribution, rotation, and retirement processes based on predefined policies and compliance requirements.

Access Controls: Enforce fine-grained access controls, authentication mechanisms, and audit trails for key usage and management activities.

Integration: Integrate with cryptographic libraries, applications, cloud services, and hardware security modules (HSMs) for seamless key operations and cryptographic functions.

4. Importance of Secure Key Management:

Data Confidentiality: Secure key management practices prevent unauthorized access to encryption keys, ensuring data confidentiality and preventing data breaches.

Data Integrity: Protecting keys from tampering or unauthorized modification maintains the integrity of encryption processes and prevents cryptographic attacks.

Compliance and Trust: Adhering to secure key management practices and regulatory standards builds trust with stakeholders, customers, and regulatory bodies regarding data protection and security controls.

Cryptographic Resilience: Effective key management contributes to cryptographic resilience by mitigating risks associated with key compromise, insider threats, and cryptographic vulnerabilities.

Conclusion:

Key management is a foundational aspect of cryptographic systems and data protection strategies, ensuring the confidentiality, integrity, and security of sensitive information. Implementing robust key management practices, leveraging key management systems (KMS), adhering to standards and compliance requirements, and continuous monitoring contribute to a strong security posture and effective data protection mechanisms in modern cybersecurity environments. Secure key management is a shared responsibility across organizations, cryptographic service providers, and security professionals to mitigate cryptographic risks and safeguard critical data assets against evolving threats.

Chapter: Data Encryption

Data encryption is a fundamental cybersecurity technique used to protect sensitive information by converting it into ciphertext, which can only be decrypted with the appropriate encryption key. This chapter explores data encryption principles, techniques, algorithms, modes, and best practices for securing data at rest and in transit.

1. Principles of Data Encryption:
Data encryption employs mathematical algorithms to transform plaintext data into ciphertext, rendering it unreadable without the correct decryption key. Key principles include confidentiality, integrity, authenticity, and non-repudiation.

2. Encryption Techniques:

Symmetric Encryption: Uses a single shared key for encryption and decryption processes. Prominent algorithms include AES (Advanced Encryption Standard), DES (Data Encryption Standard), and 3DES (Triple DES).
Asymmetric Encryption: Utilizes a pair of keys (public and private) for encryption and decryption. RSA, ECC (Elliptic Curve Cryptography), and Diffie-Hellman key exchange are common asymmetric encryption techniques.
3. Encryption Algorithms:

AES (Advanced Encryption Standard): Widely adopted symmetric encryption algorithm with key lengths of 128, 192, or 256 bits for strong encryption.
RSA (Rivest-Shamir-Adleman): Popular asymmetric encryption algorithm for secure key exchange, digital signatures, and encryption in protocols like TLS/SSL.

4. Modes of Operation:

Encryption modes define how encryption algorithms encrypt plaintext data into ciphertext. Common modes include ECB (Electronic Codebook), CBC (Cipher Block Chaining), and GCM (Galois/Counter Mode), each offering unique properties for data encryption.

5. Data Encryption Standards:

Adherence to encryption standards and protocols such as FIPS 140-2 (Federal Information Processing Standards) for cryptographic modules, TLS/SSL for secure communication, and AES encryption for data protection ensures interoperability, compliance, and security best practices.

6. Best Practices for Data Encryption:

Key Management: Generate strong encryption keys, securely distribute keys, rotate keys regularly, and use key management systems (KMS) or hardware security modules (HSMs) for key protection.

Data Classification: Identify and classify sensitive data to determine encryption requirements based on data sensitivity, regulatory requirements, and business needs.

Encryption at Rest: Encrypt data stored in databases, files, and storage devices using encryption algorithms and secure key management practices to protect against unauthorized access and data breaches.

Encryption in Transit: Use encrypted communication protocols (TLS/SSL, VPNs) for secure data transmission over networks, preventing data interception and eavesdropping attacks.

Compliance: Adhere to industry standards (PCI DSS, HIPAA, GDPR) and regulatory requirements for data encryption, privacy, and security controls.

Conclusion:

Data encryption plays a vital role in safeguarding sensitive information, ensuring data confidentiality, integrity, and privacy in modern cybersecurity environments. Implementing robust encryption techniques, adhering to encryption standards, managing encryption keys securely, and integrating encryption into data protection strategies are essential practices for organizations to mitigate data risks, comply with regulations, and maintain trust with stakeholders and customers regarding data security and privacy. Encryption should be part of a comprehensive security approach encompassing risk management, threat detection, incident response, and ongoing security awareness efforts.

Chapter: Encryption Software

Encryption software plays a crucial role in implementing data security measures by providing tools and algorithms for encrypting and decrypting sensitive information. This chapter explores different types of encryption software, their features, use cases, and considerations for selecting and implementing encryption solutions in cybersecurity strategies.

1. Types of Encryption Software:

File Encryption Software: Encrypts individual files or folders, providing on-the-fly encryption and decryption for data stored on local drives or removable media. Examples include VeraCrypt, BitLocker (Windows), and FileVault (macOS).

Disk Encryption Software: Encrypts entire disk volumes or partitions, protecting all data stored on a disk. Disk encryption solutions like BitLocker, FileVault, and Symantec Endpoint Encryption secure data at rest and require authentication during boot-up.

Email Encryption Software: Enables secure email communication by encrypting email messages and attachments to protect sensitive information during transmission. Popular email encryption tools include PGP (Pretty Good Privacy), GPG (GNU Privacy Guard), and S/MIME (Secure/Multipurpose Internet Mail Extensions).

Network Encryption Software: Secures data transmitted over networks by encrypting network traffic using protocols like TLS/SSL for web traffic, IPsec for VPNs, and SSH for secure remote access. Network encryption tools include OpenSSL, OpenVPN, and Cisco AnyConnect.

2. Features of Encryption Software:

Encryption Algorithms: Supports various encryption algorithms such as AES (Advanced Encryption Standard), RSA, ECC, and others for data protection.

Key Management: Provides features for secure key generation, storage, distribution, rotation, and revocation to manage encryption keys effectively.

Authentication: Integrates authentication mechanisms like passwords, biometrics, smart cards, or tokens to control access to encrypted data or decryption keys.

Compliance: Offers features to comply with industry standards (PCI DSS, HIPAA, GDPR) and regulatory requirements for data encryption, privacy, and security controls.

Ease of Use: User-friendly interfaces, automated encryption/decryption processes, and seamless integration with existing workflows enhance usability and adoption.

3. Use Cases of Encryption Software:

Data Protection: Encrypt sensitive files, databases, and storage devices to protect against unauthorized access, data breaches, and theft.

Secure Communication: Encrypt emails, chat messages, and file transfers to ensure confidentiality, integrity, and authenticity in digital communications.

Cloud Security: Encrypt data before uploading to cloud storage services (e.g., Dropbox, Google Drive) using client-side encryption tools or cloud encryption gateways.

Compliance Requirements: Implement encryption solutions to meet regulatory requirements for data protection, privacy, and security standards in specific industries (finance, healthcare, etc.).

4. Considerations for Choosing Encryption Software:

Security Strength: Evaluate encryption algorithms, key lengths, and cryptographic protocols supported by the software to ensure robust data security.

Key Management: Assess key management features for secure key generation, storage, and lifecycle management, including key rotation and revocation capabilities.

Integration: Consider compatibility with existing systems, applications, and platforms to seamlessly integrate encryption functionalities into workflows.

Scalability and Performance: Ensure the software can scale to meet growing encryption demands without compromising performance or introducing latency.

User Experience: Look for intuitive interfaces, user-friendly encryption workflows, and automation capabilities to streamline encryption processes and user adoption.

Conclusion:

Encryption software plays a critical role in protecting sensitive data, securing communication channels, and ensuring compliance with data protection regulations. Organizations should carefully evaluate encryption software based on security features, key management capabilities, integration possibilities, scalability, and user experience to implement effective data encryption strategies aligned with their cybersecurity objectives and regulatory requirements. Combined with robust encryption practices, secure key management, and user awareness, encryption software forms an essential component of comprehensive data protection frameworks in modern cybersecurity landscapes.

Chapter: Network Security

Network security is paramount in safeguarding networks, systems, and data from unauthorized access, cyberattacks, and data breaches. This chapter explores key aspects of network security, common threats, security measures, and best practices to ensure robust network protection in today's digital landscape.

1. Importance of Network Security:

Data Protection: Securing sensitive data, intellectual property, and confidential information from unauthorized access, theft, or tampering.

System Integrity: Preventing unauthorized modifications, malware infections, and system disruptions that can compromise system integrity and functionality.

Availability: Ensuring network services, resources, and applications are available and accessible to authorized users while defending against denial-of-service (DoS) attacks and downtime.

Compliance: Meeting regulatory requirements (PCI DSS, HIPAA, GDPR) and industry standards for data protection, privacy, and cybersecurity controls.

2. Common Network Security Threats:

Malware: Viruses, worms, Trojans, ransomware, and other malicious software targeting network devices, endpoints, and data.

Phishing and Social Engineering: Deceptive techniques to trick users into disclosing sensitive information, passwords, or installing malware.

Denial-of-Service (DoS) Attacks: Overwhelming network resources, servers, or applications to disrupt services and cause downtime.

Insider Threats: Malicious or negligent actions by employees, contractors, or trusted insiders that compromise network security and data confidentiality.

Unauthorized Access: Intrusions, unauthorized logins, exploitation of vulnerabilities, and privilege escalation leading to unauthorized access to networks or systems.

3. Network Security Measures:

Firewalls: Hardware or software-based firewalls inspect and filter network traffic based on predefined rules to block unauthorized access and malicious traffic.

Intrusion Detection and Prevention Systems (IDPS): Monitor network traffic, detect suspicious activities, and prevent intrusions or attacks in real-time.

Virtual Private Networks (VPNs): Encrypt network traffic between remote users/devices and corporate networks to ensure secure remote access and data privacy.

Network Segmentation: Dividing networks into separate segments or subnetworks with access controls to contain and mitigate security risks and limit lateral movement of threats.

Access Control: Implementing least privilege principles, strong authentication mechanisms (e.g., multi-factor authentication), and access controls to restrict unauthorized access to network resources.

Encryption: Encrypting sensitive data, communications, and network traffic using cryptographic protocols (e.g., TLS/SSL) to protect against eavesdropping and data interception.

4. Best Practices for Network Security:

Regular Security Audits: Conducting periodic network security assessments, vulnerability scans, and penetration testing to identify and remediate security weaknesses.

Patch Management: Applying security patches, updates, and firmware upgrades promptly to mitigate known vulnerabilities in network devices, servers, and software.

User Education: Providing cybersecurity training, awareness programs, and best practices to educate users about phishing threats, password hygiene, and security protocols.

Incident Response: Developing and implementing incident response plans, procedures, and protocols to detect, respond to, and recover from security incidents and breaches promptly.

Secure Configurations: Configuring network devices, routers, switches, and firewalls with secure settings, disabling unnecessary services, and using strong encryption and authentication protocols.

Backup and Recovery: Implementing regular data backups, testing backup integrity, and establishing data recovery procedures to mitigate data loss due to cyberattacks, disasters, or system failures.

Conclusion:
Network security is a multifaceted discipline crucial for protecting organizational assets, ensuring business continuity, and maintaining trust with stakeholders and customers. By implementing a layered approach to network security, leveraging advanced security technologies, conducting regular risk assessments, and fostering a security-aware culture, organizations can mitigate network security threats, minimize cybersecurity risks, and build resilient network infrastructures capable of withstanding evolving cyber threats in today's interconnected world.

Chapter: Cryptography Basics

Cryptography is the science and art of securing communication and data through encryption techniques. This chapter explores the fundamental concepts of cryptography, encryption algorithms, cryptographic keys, and common cryptographic protocols essential for understanding modern cybersecurity practices.

1. What is Cryptography?
Cryptography is the practice of converting plaintext information into ciphertext using algorithms and keys to ensure confidentiality, integrity, authentication, and non-repudiation in data communication and storage.

2. Encryption and Decryption:

Encryption: The process of converting plaintext data into ciphertext using an encryption algorithm and an encryption key.
Decryption: The reverse process of converting ciphertext back to plaintext using a decryption algorithm and the corresponding decryption key.
3. Types of Cryptography:

Symmetric Cryptography: Uses a single secret key for both encryption and decryption. Examples include AES (Advanced Encryption Standard), DES (Data Encryption Standard), and 3DES (Triple DES).
Asymmetric Cryptography: Uses a pair of public and private keys for encryption and decryption. Examples include RSA (Rivest-Shamir-Adleman) and ECC (Elliptic Curve Cryptography).
4. Cryptographic Keys:

Symmetric Keys: Shared secret keys used in symmetric encryption algorithms for both encryption and decryption processes.

Public and Private Keys: Asymmetric encryption uses a public key for encryption and a private key for decryption, ensuring secure key exchange and digital signatures.

5. Cryptographic Algorithms:

AES (Advanced Encryption Standard): A widely-used symmetric encryption algorithm with key lengths of 128, 192, or 256 bits, known for its security and efficiency.

RSA (Rivest-Shamir-Adleman): An asymmetric encryption algorithm used for secure key exchange, digital signatures, and encryption in protocols like TLS/SSL.

6. Cryptographic Protocols:

TLS/SSL (Transport Layer Security/Secure Sockets Layer): Protocols used to secure communication channels over the internet through encryption, authentication, and data integrity verification.

IPsec (Internet Protocol Security): A suite of protocols for securing IP communications through encryption, authentication, and key management for VPNs and network security.

7. Cryptographic Hash Functions:

SHA-256 (Secure Hash Algorithm 256-bit): A cryptographic hash function that generates a fixed-size hash value from input data, used for data integrity verification and digital signatures.

8. Cryptographic Applications:

Data Encryption: Securing sensitive data at rest (storage encryption) and in transit (communication encryption) to prevent unauthorized access and data breaches.

Digital Signatures: Verifying the authenticity, integrity, and non-repudiation of digital documents and messages using cryptographic hash functions and public-key cryptography.
Key Exchange: Securely exchanging symmetric encryption keys using asymmetric encryption algorithms and protocols like Diffie-Hellman key exchange.

Conclusion:

Understanding cryptography basics is fundamental to implementing robust security measures in modern IT environments. Cryptography ensures data confidentiality, integrity, authentication, and non-repudiation, forming the backbone of secure communication, data protection, and cryptographic protocols used in cybersecurity. By leveraging cryptographic algorithms, keys, protocols, and best practices, organizations can establish secure communication channels, protect sensitive information, and mitigate cybersecurity risks effectively in today's interconnected digital world.

Chapter: Encryption Principles

Encryption principles form the foundation of secure communication and data protection in modern cybersecurity. This chapter delves into key encryption principles, including confidentiality, integrity, authenticity, and non-repudiation, and explores how encryption technologies uphold these principles to safeguard sensitive information.

1. Confidentiality:
Confidentiality ensures that only authorized parties can access and read sensitive data. Encryption achieves confidentiality by converting plaintext data into ciphertext, making it unreadable to unauthorized entities without the decryption key. Strong encryption algorithms such as AES (Advanced Encryption Standard) and RSA (Rivest-Shamir-Adleman) uphold confidentiality by ensuring that encrypted data remains secure even if intercepted.

2. Integrity:
Integrity ensures that data remains unchanged and unaltered during transmission or storage. Encryption technologies use cryptographic hash functions and digital signatures to verify data integrity. Hash functions generate unique hash values for data, and any modification to the data results in a different hash value, detecting tampering. Digital signatures provide authentication and integrity by using public-key cryptography to verify the sender's identity and ensure data integrity through signature verification.

3. Authenticity:

Authenticity verifies the identity of parties involved in data communication or transactions. Public-key cryptography, a core principle in ensuring authenticity, uses asymmetric encryption to establish secure communication channels and verify the authenticity of digital signatures. Digital certificates issued by trusted Certificate Authorities (CAs) further validate the authenticity of entities, websites, or digital communications, enhancing trust and security in online interactions.

4. Non-Repudiation:
Non-repudiation prevents parties from denying their actions or transactions. Digital signatures play a crucial role in providing non-repudiation by binding a signature to a specific message or document. Once a digital signature is applied using the signer's private key, it can be verified with the corresponding public key, proving the authenticity of the signer, and ensuring non-repudiation of the signed content.

5. Encryption Algorithms and Keys:
Encryption algorithms like AES, RSA, and ECC implement these encryption principles by using strong mathematical techniques to encrypt and decrypt data securely. Symmetric encryption employs a shared secret key for encryption and decryption, ensuring confidentiality, while asymmetric encryption uses key pairs (public and private keys) for secure key exchange, digital signatures, and authentication, supporting principles like authenticity and non-repudiation.

6. Implementation Considerations:

Key Management: Secure generation, distribution, rotation, and protection of encryption keys are critical for maintaining confidentiality and integrity.

Cryptographic Standards: Adherence to recognized cryptographic standards and protocols (e.g., TLS/SSL for secure communication) ensures interoperability, security, and compliance with industry regulations.

Secure Communication Channels: Implementing encryption protocols (e.g., IPsec, TLS/SSL) and secure configurations in networks and systems protects data during transmission and prevents unauthorized access.

Conclusion:

Encryption principles guide the design and implementation of encryption technologies to uphold confidentiality, integrity, authenticity, and non-repudiation in data protection and secure communication. Understanding these principles helps organizations deploy robust encryption strategies, select appropriate encryption algorithms and keys, and ensure secure data handling practices across various cybersecurity domains, ultimately enhancing data security, privacy, and trust in digital interactions.

Chapter: Secure Coding Practices

Secure coding practices are essential for developing software applications that are resilient to cyber threats and vulnerabilities. This chapter explores key principles, techniques, and guidelines for writing secure code to prevent common security vulnerabilities and protect software systems from exploitation.

1. Principle of Least Privilege:
Follow the principle of least privilege by ensuring that code and users have only the minimum permissions necessary to perform their functions. Limiting access rights reduces the attack surface and minimizes the impact of potential security breaches.

2. Input Validation and Sanitization:
Validate and sanitize all user inputs to prevent injection attacks such as SQL injection, cross-site scripting (XSS), and command injection. Use input validation techniques like white-listing, regular expressions, and parameterized queries to filter and sanitize input data.

3. Avoiding Hard-Coded Secrets:
Do not hard-code sensitive information such as passwords, API keys, or cryptographic keys directly into source code. Use secure storage mechanisms (e.g., environment variables, secure vaults) and configuration management practices to manage secrets securely.

4. Secure Authentication and Authorization:

Implement strong authentication mechanisms (e.g., multi-factor authentication, OAuth) to verify user identities securely. Apply proper authorization checks to ensure that users or processes have appropriate permissions before accessing sensitive resources or executing privileged operations.

5. Secure Cryptographic Practices:
Use well-tested cryptographic libraries and algorithms for encryption, hashing, and digital signatures. Follow cryptographic best practices such as using strong key lengths, secure random number generation, and avoiding weak algorithms or deprecated cryptographic protocols.

6. Error Handling and Logging:
Implement robust error handling mechanisms to gracefully handle exceptions and errors without exposing sensitive information or system details to users. Log security-relevant events and anomalies for monitoring, analysis, and incident response purposes.

7. Secure Communication Protocols:
Use secure communication protocols (e.g., TLS/SSL) to encrypt data transmitted over networks and protect against eavesdropping, man-in-the-middle attacks, and data tampering. Verify server certificates and enforce secure communication practices in client-server interactions.

8. Regular Security Testing:
Conduct regular security testing such as code reviews, static code analysis, dynamic application security testing (DAST), and penetration testing to identify and remediate security vulnerabilities early in the software development lifecycle (SDLC).

9. Secure Dependencies and Libraries:

Regularly update and patch dependencies, libraries, and third-party components used in your software to mitigate vulnerabilities and security risks. Monitor for security advisories and apply security patches promptly.

10. Security Education and Awareness:
Promote security awareness among developers, QA teams, and stakeholders through training programs, workshops, and knowledge sharing sessions. Encourage security best practices, code review practices, and adherence to secure coding standards and guidelines.

Conclusion:
Secure coding practices are crucial for building robust and resilient software applications that withstand cyber threats and protect sensitive data. By integrating security into the software development process, adopting secure coding principles and techniques, leveraging secure libraries and protocols, and fostering a security-aware culture, organizations can reduce security risks, prevent common vulnerabilities, and enhance overall cybersecurity posture across their software ecosystems. Regular security testing, code reviews, and continuous improvement efforts are integral to maintaining secure coding practices and adapting to evolving security challenges in today's dynamic threat landscape.

Chapter: Encryption in the Cloud

Encryption plays a vital role in ensuring data confidentiality and security, especially in cloud computing environments where data is stored, processed, and transmitted across distributed networks. This chapter explores the challenges, strategies, and best practices for implementing encryption effectively in cloud environments to protect sensitive data from unauthorized access and breaches.

1. Cloud Security Challenges:

Data Privacy: Ensuring confidentiality and privacy of sensitive data stored in cloud repositories.
Data Integrity: Preventing unauthorized modifications or tampering of data during storage or transmission.
Data Compliance: Adhering to regulatory requirements (GDPR, HIPAA, etc.) for data protection and privacy in cloud environments.
Shared Responsibility: Understanding the shared responsibility model between cloud service providers (CSPs) and customers for securing data and infrastructure.
2. Encryption Types in Cloud Environments:

Data-at-Rest Encryption: Encrypting data stored in cloud databases, storage services (e.g., Amazon S3, Azure Blob Storage), and virtual disks using encryption algorithms such as AES (Advanced Encryption Standard).
Data-in-Transit Encryption: Securing data transmitted over networks between cloud services, users, and devices using protocols like TLS/SSL, IPsec, and VPNs to prevent eavesdropping and interception.

Database Encryption: Encrypting sensitive data fields within databases (e.g., credit card numbers, personal information) using database encryption features or application-level encryption to protect against unauthorized access.

3. Key Management in Cloud Encryption:

Key Generation: Securely generating encryption keys using strong cryptographic algorithms and random number generators.

Key Storage: Safely storing encryption keys in cloud key management services (KMS), hardware security modules (HSMs), or secure vaults with access controls and audit trails.

Key Rotation: Regularly rotating encryption keys to limit exposure and enhance security in case of key compromise or vulnerabilities.

Key Custodianship: Defining roles, responsibilities, and access controls for managing encryption keys across cloud environments based on the principle of least privilege.

4. Encryption Best Practices for Cloud Security:

Data Classification: Identify and classify data based on sensitivity levels to determine encryption requirements and access controls.

End-to-End Encryption: Implement end-to-end encryption (E2EE) for applications and services to ensure data remains encrypted throughout its lifecycle, from creation to storage and transmission.

Multi-Layered Security: Combine encryption with other security measures such as access controls, identity management, intrusion detection, and logging for comprehensive cloud security.

Compliance and Standards: Adhere to industry standards, regulatory requirements, and cloud security best practices for encryption, key management, and data protection in cloud environments.

Regular Audits and Monitoring: Conduct regular security audits, vulnerability assessments, and encryption audits to monitor and validate the effectiveness of encryption controls and security measures.

5. Cloud Encryption Services and Tools:

Cloud Provider Encryption Services: Utilize built-in encryption features and services offered by cloud providers (AWS KMS, Azure Key Vault, Google Cloud KMS) for managing encryption keys and securing data.

Third-Party Encryption Tools: Leverage third-party encryption tools, libraries, and solutions for additional encryption capabilities, cross-cloud encryption, and integration with existing security frameworks.

Conclusion:

Encryption is a fundamental component of cloud security strategies, ensuring data confidentiality, integrity, and compliance in cloud computing environments. By implementing encryption best practices, leveraging cloud encryption services, managing encryption keys securely, and staying updated with evolving security trends and standards, organizations can strengthen their cloud security posture, mitigate data risks, and build trust with customers and stakeholders regarding data protection and privacy in the cloud.

Chapter: Quantum Encryption

Quantum encryption represents a revolutionary approach to secure communication that leverages principles of quantum mechanics to offer unprecedented levels of security against conventional cryptographic attacks. This chapter explores the concepts, principles, challenges, and potential of quantum encryption in transforming cybersecurity.

1. Understanding Quantum Encryption:
Quantum encryption harnesses the principles of quantum mechanics, such as superposition and entanglement, to encrypt and transmit information in a quantum-secure manner. Unlike classical encryption, which relies on mathematical complexity, quantum encryption utilizes quantum properties to achieve unbreakable encryption keys.

2. Quantum Key Distribution (QKD):
Quantum Key Distribution is a core concept in quantum encryption that enables two parties to establish a shared encryption key securely. QKD protocols, such as BB84 and E91, use quantum properties to detect eavesdropping attempts, ensuring the secrecy of the key exchange process.

3. Quantum Cryptography vs. Classical Cryptography:

Key Distribution: Quantum cryptography provides provably secure key distribution through QKD, while classical cryptography relies on complex mathematical algorithms vulnerable to quantum attacks (e.g., Shor's algorithm for factoring large numbers, which threatens RSA encryption).

Security Assumptions: Quantum cryptography relies on the laws of physics (quantum mechanics) for security assumptions, offering information-theoretic security guarantees, unlike classical cryptography based on computational complexity assumptions.

Post-Quantum Cryptography: With the advent of quantum computing, post-quantum cryptography research aims to develop cryptographic algorithms resistant to quantum attacks, bridging the gap between classical and quantum cryptographic systems.

4. Quantum Encryption Challenges:

Technology Maturity: Quantum encryption technologies are still in the early stages of development and deployment, requiring advancements in hardware, protocols, and standards for practical implementation.

Key Distribution Distance: QKD systems face limitations in key distribution distance due to factors such as quantum signal degradation over optical fibers, requiring quantum repeaters or satellite-based quantum communication for long-distance secure communication.

Integration Complexity: Integrating quantum encryption systems with existing classical cryptographic infrastructures and protocols poses integration challenges and compatibility considerations.

5. Quantum Encryption Applications:

Secure Communication: Quantum encryption ensures secure communication channels for sensitive data transmission, offering protection against quantum computing-enabled attacks.

Financial Transactions: Quantum encryption enhances the security of financial transactions, digital signatures, and blockchain technologies, safeguarding against quantum attacks targeting cryptographic keys.

Government and Defense: Quantum encryption technologies find applications in secure military communications, intelligence agencies, and government sectors requiring high levels of secrecy and protection against sophisticated adversaries.

6. Future Directions and Impact:

Quantum Internet: The development of a quantum internet infrastructure integrating quantum encryption and communication protocols promises ultra-secure global communication networks resistant to quantum attacks.

Quantum-Secure Cryptography Standards: Collaborative efforts in developing quantum-safe cryptographic standards and algorithms (post-quantum cryptography) aim to mitigate risks posed by quantum computing to existing cryptographic systems.

Commercial Adoption: As quantum encryption technologies mature, commercial adoption across industries such as finance, healthcare, and telecommunications is expected, driving innovation and advancements in quantum cybersecurity.

Conclusion:

Quantum encryption represents a paradigm shift in cybersecurity, offering unparalleled levels of security and resilience against quantum-enabled attacks. While facing technological challenges and deployment complexities, ongoing research, collaborations, and investments in quantum encryption technologies pave the way for a quantum-secure future, where information can be protected with unbreakable quantum cryptographic techniques. Embracing quantum encryption principles and exploring its potential applications will be instrumental in shaping the next generation of secure communication and data protection strategies in the evolving digital landscape.

Chapter: Encryption for Beginners

Encryption forms the backbone of secure communication and data protection in today's digital world. This chapter introduces encryption concepts in a beginner-friendly manner, explaining the basics of encryption, common encryption algorithms, and practical tips for understanding and implementing encryption for personal and professional use.

1. What is Encryption?
Encryption is the process of converting plain, readable data (plaintext) into an encoded, unreadable format (ciphertext) using cryptographic algorithms and keys. The purpose of encryption is to ensure data confidentiality, preventing unauthorized access or understanding of the encrypted data.

2. Key Terms in Encryption:

Plaintext: Original, unencrypted data that you want to protect.
Ciphertext: Encrypted data generated after applying encryption algorithms to plaintext.
Encryption Algorithm: Mathematical procedures and formulas used to encrypt and decrypt data securely.
Encryption Key: Secret value used by encryption algorithms to transform plaintext into ciphertext and vice versa.
3. Types of Encryption:

Symmetric Encryption: Uses a single secret key for both encryption and decryption. Examples include AES (Advanced Encryption Standard) and DES (Data Encryption Standard).
Asymmetric Encryption: Uses a pair of public and private keys for encryption and decryption. Examples include RSA (Rivest-Shamir-Adleman) and ECC (Elliptic Curve Cryptography).

4. How Encryption Works:

Encryption Process: The plaintext is combined with the encryption key using an encryption algorithm, resulting in ciphertext.

Decryption Process: The ciphertext is combined with the decryption key (for symmetric encryption) or the recipient's private key (for asymmetric encryption) using a decryption algorithm to retrieve the original plaintext.

5. Common Encryption Algorithms:

AES (Advanced Encryption Standard): Widely used symmetric encryption algorithm known for its security and efficiency.

RSA (Rivest-Shamir-Adleman): Popular asymmetric encryption algorithm used for secure key exchange, digital signatures, and encryption.

6. Practical Encryption Tips:

Use Strong Passwords: Secure your encryption keys with strong, unique passwords or passphrases to prevent unauthorized access.

Secure Storage: Store encryption keys securely using trusted key management solutions, hardware security modules (HSMs), or secure vaults.

Regular Updates: Keep encryption software and algorithms updated to mitigate vulnerabilities and ensure strong security.

Understand Compliance: Familiarize yourself with encryption regulations and compliance standards relevant to your industry or jurisdiction (e.g., GDPR, HIPAA).

7. Encryption Tools for Beginners:

File Encryption Software: Use user-friendly encryption software such as VeraCrypt, BitLocker (Windows), or FileVault (macOS) to encrypt files and folders on your computer.

Messaging Apps: Utilize messaging apps with built-in end-to-end encryption (e.g., Signal, WhatsApp) for secure communication.
Online Services: Explore cloud storage services (e.g., Google Drive, Dropbox) with encryption options to protect your stored data.
8. Learning Resources:

Online Tutorials: Take advantage of online tutorials, courses, and resources to learn more about encryption principles, algorithms, and best practices.
Books and Guides: Refer to beginner-friendly books and guides on encryption and cybersecurity topics to deepen your understanding.
Community Forums: Engage with cybersecurity communities, forums, and discussions to ask questions, share knowledge, and stay updated on encryption trends and developments.
Conclusion:
Encryption is a powerful tool for protecting sensitive information, maintaining privacy, and enhancing cybersecurity. By understanding the basics of encryption, exploring common encryption algorithms, adopting best practices, and leveraging user-friendly encryption tools, beginners can start implementing encryption effectively in their digital activities, safeguarding their data and communications in an increasingly connected world. Continued learning and awareness of encryption concepts will empower individuals and organizations to stay secure and resilient against cyber threats.

Chapter: Bitcoin and Cryptocurrency Explained

Bitcoin and cryptocurrencies have revolutionized the financial landscape, introducing decentralized digital currencies and blockchain technology. This chapter provides an introductory overview of Bitcoin, cryptocurrency concepts, blockchain technology, and the broader impact of cryptocurrencies on finance and technology.

1. Understanding Bitcoin:
Bitcoin is the first and most well-known cryptocurrency, created in 2009 by an anonymous entity known as Satoshi Nakamoto. It operates on a decentralized peer-to-peer network without a central authority, using blockchain technology to record transactions securely.

2. Key Concepts in Cryptocurrency:

Decentralization: Cryptocurrencies operate without central control or intermediaries like banks, enabling direct peer-to-peer transactions across the network.
Blockchain: A distributed ledger technology that records all transactions in chronological order, forming a chain of blocks secured through cryptographic principles.
Cryptographic Security: Cryptography ensures the security, privacy, and integrity of cryptocurrency transactions and wallet ownership.
3. How Cryptocurrency Works:

Cryptocurrency Units: Digital tokens or coins (e.g., Bitcoin, Ethereum, Litecoin) serve as units of value in cryptocurrency networks.
Wallets: Digital wallets store cryptographic keys used to access and manage cryptocurrency holdings securely.

Transactions: Cryptocurrency transactions involve transferring digital assets between wallet addresses on the blockchain, verified by network consensus mechanisms (e.g., proof-of-work, proof-of-stake).

4. Popular Cryptocurrencies:

Bitcoin (BTC): The pioneering cryptocurrency, often referred to as digital gold, valued for its scarcity, decentralization, and store of value properties.

Ethereum (ETH): Known for its smart contract capabilities, Ethereum enables developers to build decentralized applications (dApps) and execute programmable transactions.

Altcoins: Thousands of alternative cryptocurrencies (altcoins) exist, offering various features, use cases, and blockchain innovations beyond Bitcoin and Ethereum (e.g., Ripple/XRP, Litecoin, Cardano).

5. Blockchain Technology:

Immutable Ledger: Blockchain records transactions in blocks linked cryptographically, ensuring transparency, auditability, and tamper-resistant data.

Decentralized Consensus: Consensus algorithms (e.g., proof-of-work, proof-of-stake) validate and secure transactions without central control, promoting trust in decentralized networks.

Smart Contracts: Self-executing contracts coded on blockchain platforms like Ethereum automate agreement terms and transactions, reducing intermediaries and enhancing efficiency.

6. Cryptocurrency Use Cases:

Digital Payments: Cryptocurrencies facilitate borderless and low-cost peer-to-peer transactions globally, offering financial inclusion and alternative payment solutions.

Tokenization: Blockchain enables tokenization of assets (real estate, artwork, securities) into digital tokens, enhancing liquidity, fractional ownership, and asset tracking.

Decentralized Finance (DeFi): DeFi platforms leverage blockchain and smart contracts for decentralized lending, borrowing, trading, and yield farming, disrupting traditional finance.

Non-Fungible Tokens (NFTs): Unique digital assets represented as NFTs on blockchains like Ethereum, enabling ownership and trading of digital art, collectibles, and virtual assets.

7. Risks and Challenges:

Volatility: Cryptocurrency prices can experience extreme volatility due to market speculation, regulatory changes, and market sentiment.

Security: Risks include hacking attacks on exchanges, phishing scams, wallet vulnerabilities, and smart contract exploits.

Regulatory Environment: Cryptocurrency regulations vary globally, impacting adoption, taxation, and legality of crypto-related activities.

8. Future Trends and Adoption:

Institutional Investment: Growing institutional interest and adoption of cryptocurrencies as investment assets and hedge against inflation.

Central Bank Digital Currencies (CBDCs): Exploration and development of digital currencies by central banks for national payment systems and monetary policy.

Blockchain Innovations: Continued advancements in blockchain technology, scalability solutions (e.g., layer 2 protocols), and interoperability standards for blockchain networks.

Conclusion:

Bitcoin and cryptocurrencies have reshaped financial paradigms, offering decentralized, borderless, and innovative solutions for digital assets, payments, and decentralized applications. Understanding the fundamentals of cryptocurrency, blockchain technology, use cases, risks, and emerging trends is essential for navigating the evolving landscape of digital finance, investment opportunities, and technological disruptions in the years ahead. Continued research, education, and responsible participation in cryptocurrency ecosystems empower individuals and businesses to harness the potential benefits while managing risks in this transformative era of digital currencies and decentralized technologies.

www.ingramcontent.com/pod-product-compliance
Lightning Source LLC
Chambersburg PA
CBHW052201220526
45471CB00004B/1768